Strategic Teaching and Learning:
Cognitive Instruction in the Content Areas

Strategic Teaching and Learning:

Cognitive Instruction in the Content Areas

Edited by
Beau Fly Jones
Annemarie Sullivan Palincsar
Donna Sederburg Ogle
Eileen Glynn Carr

Association for Supervision and Curriculum Development
in cooperation with the
North Central Regional Educational Laboratory

This book was produced by the Association for Supervision and Curriculum Development in cooperation with the North Central Regional Educational Laboratory. All rights reserved.

ASCD
125 N. West Street
Alexandria, VA 22314-2798
Telephone 703-549-9110

NCREL
295 Emroy Avenue
Elmhurst, IL 60126
Telephone 312-941-7677

Executive Editor: Ronald S. Brandt
Manager of Publications: Nancy Carter Modrak
Art Director: Al Way

ASCD Stock Number: 611-87030
ISBN: 0-87120-147-X
Library of Congress Catalog Card Number: 87-071387

$10.00

Acknowledgments

I t is a fundamental assumption of this book that what we choose to teach in the classroom should be an interaction of what we know about the variables of instruction, learning, assessment, and contextual factors. This assumption has driven our quest as individuals and groups to develop an instructional framework for effective cognitive instruction through four successive and related works.

Parts of this framework were first developed by Jones, Friedman, Tinzmann, and Cox (1984) in a manual entitled *Context-Driven Comprehension Instruction: A Model for Army Training Literature*, for the U.S. Army Research Institute for the Social and Behavioral Sciences (see also Jones 1985). The framework was then modified considerably by Palincsar, Ogle, Jones, and Carr (1986) for a videotape and facilitator's manual, *Teaching Reading as Thinking*. Third, Jones, Tinzmann, Friedman, and Walker (1987) applied this framework to the language arts in a book for the National Education Association, *Teaching Thinking Skills in English/Language Arts*, which focused on three key concepts: strategic learning, the importance of organizational patterns, and strategic teaching. This book applies this same model to the content areas.

We wish to acknowledge the help of many people who made this book possible. Our most outstanding debt is to the four authors who applied our model to the content areas: Charles W. Anderson, Michigan State University; Mary Montgomery Lindquist, Columbus College, Columbus, Georgia; Donna Alvermann, University of Georgia at Athens; and Richard Beach, University of Minnesota. In addition, we thank those who reviewed the first draft of this book and provided many useful comments: Patricia F. Campbell, University of Maryland and representative, National Council of Teachers of Mathematics; Joanne Capper, Executive Director, Center for Research into Practice; Sue Derber, teacher, Carl Sandberg Elementary School, Springfield, Illinois; Marie Espinada, Willow Creek Junior High School and representative of the National Education Association; Owen Hein, Department of Social Studies and the Humanities, Evanston High School, Evanston, Illinois; William Holiday, Science Teaching Center, University of Maryland; Joy Monahan, Reading Program Consultant, Orange County Public Schools, Orlando, Florida; Marlys Peters, Minnesota State Department; and Thomas Stefanek, Wisconsin Department of Public Instruction.

—The Editors

v

Foreword

This book will affect anyone who labors in behalf of students. It takes a courageous step beyond what is and why to what can be and how. *Strategic Teaching and Learning* explores the very heart of schools: the complex thinking process of teaching that enables all types of students to become successful learners. We cannot expect teachers and their supervisors to teach as they were taught and expect desirable results as well. The job of teaching is far more complex than simply delivering content. This has always been the case, but our recognition of it now represents a crucial step toward meeting our goal of achievement for all.

The new vision of teaching is one of a strategic process in which the teacher takes the central role as both planner and mediator of learning. The teacher teaches not only content but the strategies required by that content to make learning meaningful, integrated, and transferable. Teachers have a dual agenda: in each content area they must consider (1) which strategies students need in order to learn the content, and (2) how students can be helped to learn to use those strategies. Teaching becomes a delicate balance among content goals, strategies required for achieving those goals, and the experiences students bring to their learning.

The focus is on the student. When planning, teachers first set outcomes and then design instructional activities to match students' prior knowledge, motivation, and level of interest. They evaluate available materials and choose presentation strategies to link where students are with where the content is expected to take them. Throughout the process, teachers need to modify their plans continuously on the basis of feedback, striving for balance between giving students the guidance they need and the independence they desire.

Strategic Teaching and Learning considers various levels at which content can be learned. As teachers plan for instruction, they must differentiate strategies to match students' needs, helping less successful learners perform adequately and assisting high-scoring students to master and use understandings beyond those evaluated by tests.

Strategic teaching is a demanding concept. First, teachers must know the content thoroughly. Second, they must be able to assess their students' prior knowledge and learning needs. Third, they must be capable of analyzing text and other instructional materials in order to use them well in the teaching/learning effort. Finally, they must understand thinking processes appropriate for learning and using the content and be able to match them to effective presentation strategies.

This model has many implications for supervisors. We must accept the challenge to influence textbook organization and construction; develop strategic teachers through pre- and inservice staff development efforts; and provide the guidance, encouragement, and leadership for this dynamic process of teaching.

If our goal is achievement for all, then we need to embrace a broader, more encompassing definition of achievement that includes students' understanding, integration, and application of concepts taught in school. Achievement for all has been a locked door for educators. Now strategic teaching is offering a key that fits. To use it, we need to understand and accept the concept and then help our teachers and colleagues by encouraging staff development and text revision and by providing support for classroom implementation.

This book represents ASCD's suppport for these efforts.

MARCIA KALB KNOLL
ASCD President, 1987-88

Introduction

The Editors

Who Is the Audience for This Book?

Across the United States there is a ground swell of concern among teachers, administrators, policymakers, and researchers about the need to teach thinking skills. Everywhere, educators worry that students are unable to deal effectively with the thinking tasks required in an information-intensive society and that students generally are not achieving their highest potential. In response to this problem, there has been a national rush to implement recent research emerging from the thinking skills movement. The yield from this movement is rich in documented instructional strategies that focus on teaching thinking. Despite this, most approaches are content-free and often ignore the special needs of low-achieving students. In contrast, our approach applies directly to all content areas, including reading and literature, and to all students.

This book is for the community of educators responsible for improving the quality of instruction for our nation's youth. Specifically, it is for teachers and the instructional leaders who supervise them; for those who must develop staff development programs in inservice and preservice contexts; for curriculum developers in schools, state education departments, publishing houses, and the military; for policymakers who must make decisions about policies for students at risk and other instructional issues, and for researchers in content areas, instructional design, and other areas.

What Is This Book About?

In one sense, this book is about students' cognitive processing in that the instructional strategies we develop focus on teaching students how to process information and to think independently and effectively. Yet, in the final analysis, such a book must be about what Jones (1986) has called *cognitive instruction*. Speaking broadly, cognitive instruction focuses on understanding and learning how to learn as primary goals of instruction. Drawn largely from research on expert teaching and cognitive psychology, cognitive instruction includes instruction in the various dimensions of thinking such as comprehending and composing, problem solving and decision making, critical and creative thinking, and metacognition.

Although many instructional approaches apply concepts from this knowledge base and may legitimately be called cognitive instruction, the approach we take in this book is called *strategic teaching*. This concept calls attention to the role of the teacher as strategist, making decisions about the "what," "how," and "when" of teaching and learning. "What" refers to making decisions about the substance of instruction: the specific content, skills, and strategies. "How" refers to making decisions about the particular procedures needed to implement a given strategy or skill and about teaching those procedures to students. "When" refers to making decisions about the conditions under which it is appropriate to apply a given strategy or skill and about teaching students this information. Thus, making decisions about the content and the appropriate instructional strategies is at the heart of strategic teaching.

The role of the teacher in strategic teaching builds upon previous definitions of the teacher as manager and instructional leader. Yet the concept of strategic teaching focuses mainly on the role of the teacher as model and mediator. As a model, the strategic teacher demonstrates how to think through a given task, how to apply the strategies, and "what to do when you don't know what to do." As a mediator, the strategic teacher intercedes between the students and the learning environment to help students learn and grow, anticipates problems in learning and plans solutions to solve them, and guides and coaches students through the initial phases of learning to independent learning.

What differentiates strategic teaching from other approaches to cognitive instruction? In one sense, little in our framework is "new." Good teachers have been using most of the strategies in this book for years. Nevertheless, our framework has a number of distinctive features. These include the scope of our framework—it applies to all content areas and to all students; the attention to the dual agenda of teaching both content and strategies; the focus on organizational patterns and graphic outlining; the way of defining explicit strategy instruction; and, lastly, our conceptualization of learning and instruction as occurring in phases with recursive thinking.

Moreover, two resources in this book are rare in the research literature: (1) the various planning guides for each phase of instruction, and (2) detailed descriptions of expert teachers thinking aloud as they plan instruction. These resources consolidate research on learning, organizational patterns, and instruction in reading in the content areas of literature, social studies, math, and science. These resources help the teacher and curriculum specialist integrate the variables of instruction into a cohesive plan for whole sequences of instruction that extend well beyond the concept of a single lesson.

What Are the Uses of This Book?

The framework presented in this book has diverse uses. First, it *provides a common language and conceptual framework for teachers and adminis-*

trators across the disciplines. This feature encourages communication, collaboration, and coordination for planning curriculum and instruction in the different content areas. For example, if a whole school or district uses the same approach, it is much easier to coordinate staff development. Our framework also facilitates coordinating the teaching of thinking and assessment across the disciplines as well as the transfer of skills from one discipline to another. Moreover, to the extent that communication and collaboration are increased, teachers are less likely to feel isolated from each other and from the process of decision making.

Second, our approach provides teachers and students with a *repertoire of teaching/learning strategies* for immediate application as well as for long-term use. That is, the instructional strategies, planning guides, and thinking-aloud models can be applied directly and immediately in the classroom using existing materials; thus, educators can use our approach without abandoning time-tested instructional materials and strategies. At the same time, curriculum developers can use this approach to create new curriculum objectives and instructional materials.

Third, many of the teaching/learning strategies discussed in this book *truly integrate reading, writing, and thinking within the various content areas.* Many inservice programs for teaching reading, writing, and thinking across the curriculum in fact teach these processes separately within a given content area. That is, programs for reading in the content areas may be entirely different from programs focusing on writing or other thinking processes, and teachers may not be trained to integrate reading, writing, and thinking for specific school tasks. Strategic teaching is devised to help teachers integrate reading, writing, and other thinking processes for specific sequences of instruction within each content area and across the various subject areas.

Finally, strategic teaching is *intended to be used with all students so that both high- and low-achieving students may benefit from the same instructional strategies.* Levin (1987) argued that the reform movement has systematically neglected educationally disadvantaged students. He thinks this is so in part because the special needs of students at risk are often ignored in planning considerations and in part because existing interventions have inconsistent assumptions. Particularly damaging is the widespread practice of reserving cognitive instruction for teaching high-achieving students, thereby allotting basic skills instruction to low-achieving students. This practice deprives such students of the very thing they need most.

Our framework addresses this problem directly. To explain, there are many features in this framework that facilitate learning for high- and low-achieving students. These features include review, linking new information to prior knowledge, brainstorming and thinking aloud, in-depth processing through graphic outlining, summarizing, scaffolded instruction, and explicit strategy instruction. We hope that teachers and others can use this framework to justify policies to provide cognitive instruction for low-achieving students.

How Is This Book Organized?

The book is organized into two parts. Part I, written by the editors, describes our working conclusions about learning and instruction respectively and provides generic planning guides for identifying appropriate thinking processes, organizational patterns, and instructional strategies. We propose in Part I that these planning guides are generic in that teachers and administrators may use them to sequence curriculum and instruction in the various language arts and in the content areas for each phase of instruction: preparation for learning, presentation of the content, and application and integration. The remainder of the book is essentially a test of that proposal. We asked prominent content researchers to apply our framework to their respective areas: Charles Anderson in science, Donna Alvermann in social studies, Mary Lindquist in mathematics, and Richard Beach in literature. Basically, we asked each content specialist three questions:

1. Is the research presented in Part I of this book consistent with research in your specific content area?

2. To what extent can you apply our framework to instruction in your content area?

3. What adaptations, if any, need to be made to teach low- and high-achieving students so that all students will benefit from cognitive instruction?

Each chapter in Part II contains guidelines for planning that are essentially adaptations of the generic planning guides in Part I. These adaptations serve as examples for teachers in the various content areas.

References

Jones, B. F. "Addressing Quality and Equality Through Cognitive Instruction." *Educational Leadership* 43 (April 1986): 4-12.

Levin, H. M. "Accelerated Schools for Disadvantaged Students." *Educational Leadership* 44 (March 1987): 19-21.

Part I

A Framework for Strategic Teaching

The Editors

1 Learning and Thinking

Why does a book on teaching begin with a chapter on learning? Several strands of research suggest that what people think about how students learn has a lot to do with what is taught in the classroom and how it is taught. Consider research on expert teaching, for example. Several studies suggest that effective teachers anticipate how students will respond to specific content and what problems they will have (e.g., Leinhardt 1986). For examples of strategies that utilize research on learning, we might look at some of the more successful training studies such as Schoenfeld's (1985) efforts to teach problem solving or Palincsar's method of reciprocal teaching (Palincsar and Brown 1984), in which students learn to monitor and direct their own learning. A large part of what makes these studies special is that the instructional methods they use mirror assumptions about learning. Finally, we think back to the number of criticisms of classroom instruction and instructional materials as being ineffective because they did not reflect recent research on learning (e.g., Durkin 1978-79; Osborn, Jones, and Stein 1985).

Additionally, a fundamental tenet of developing effective teaching methods is that instruction *should* reflect what is known about learning (Brown, Campione, and Day 1981). That is, if there is convincing evidence that performance can be modified by explicit strategy instruction, then as teachers, we would want to include this instruction in our lesson plans. This does not mean that

3

teachers should try to include everything "that research says" in their lesson plans or curriculums, or that research can provide the only criteria for lesson planning. To the contrary, good lesson plans usually reflect a rich blend of teacher experience and research. What is important, however, is that one's vision of education should include an understanding of how the best students and the poorest students learn so that this knowledge can be used to improve educational opportunities for all students.

This chapter articulates six related assumptions or propositions about how students learn that have critical implications for instruction (see Figure 1.1). These assumptions do not seek to be comprehensive. Rather, we have selected them for the soundness of the research base that supports them as well as for their educational significance. Chapter 2 then discusses the implications of these assumptions for instruction.

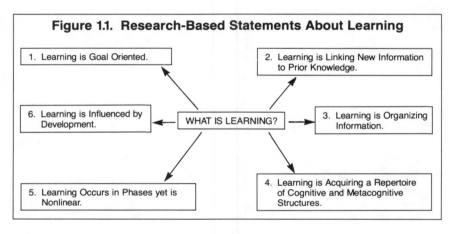

Figure 1.1. Research-Based Statements About Learning

1. Learning is Goal Oriented.

2. Learning is Linking New Information to Prior Knowledge.

6. Learning is Influenced by Development.

WHAT IS LEARNING?

3. Learning is Organizing Information.

5. Learning Occurs in Phases yet is Nonlinear.

4. Learning is Acquiring a Repertoire of Cognitive and Metacognitive Structures.

Assumption 1: Learning is Goal Oriented.

Constructing Meaning and Independent Learning

It is rare to have consensus in any discipline, especially in education. Yet there is an increasing consensus among researchers and educators in various fields of inquiry that learning is goal oriented (e.g., Resnick 1984). Particularly, there seems to be increasing agreement that the skilled learner strives to reach two goals: to understand the meaning of the tasks at hand and to regulate his or her own learning. This vision comes in part from research on cognition and in part from research on metacognition (thinking about and controlling the process of learning). In reading, for example, the model reader works actively to construct or figure out the meaning of what is read and to monitor understanding of the text at any given time (Brown 1985, Pearson 1985). In math, the expert problem solver seeks to understand not only "what to do and why" (Burns 1986) but also "what to do when you do not know what to do."

In addition to these "global" goals, the model learner may have any number of task-specific goals for a given learning context. That is, a learner may set substantive goals such as understanding a particular plot, as well as strategic goals such as learning how to summarize well or developing strategies for dealing with comprehension failure. These specific purposes for engaging in learning are powerful incentives for learning in a given situation, and they help the learner focus on what is important (Mayer 1984, Paris and Winograd in progress).

The "New" Definition of Learning

The emphasis on the importance of constructing meaning and on independent learning is hardly new to many educators. Yet it is new in educational history in that it contrasts sharply with previous understandings of how students learn. Earlier approaches assumed that learning was essentially a matter of responding to the information that was given. Reading, for example, was assumed to be a passive activity, happening largely as a result of decoding and learning the meaning of individual words. The goal of reading therefore was to "approximate" the text (Pearson 1985). There was also a widespread assumption that intelligence was relatively unmodifiable either by schools or by the efforts of the individual to control his or her own learning (Jensen 1969).

It is relatively new in educational theory to conceptualize learning as thinking, that is, as using prior knowledge and specific strategies to understand the ideas in a text as a whole or the elements of a problem as a whole. It is also fairly new to assume that schools do make a difference (Edmonds 1982), that the performance of low-achieving students is modifiable by providing appropriate instructional experiences (Feuerstein 1980, Hunt 1972), and that we can teach students to monitor and control their own performances (Brown 1980).

This new portrait of the model learner is perhaps best expressed in *Becoming a Nation of Readers* (Anderson, Hiebert, Scott, and Wilkinson 1985), a political statement as much as a presentation of research. Appointed to represent the consensus of recent research on reading, the authors portray the model reader as active, strategic, planful, and constructive in linking the new information to prior knowledge.

Significantly, each of these descriptive phrases pervades the literature on cognition and metacognition in areas such as problem solving in math and science (Schoenfeld 1985, Silver 1985), thinking (Bransford, Sherwood, Vye, and

5

Rieser 1986; Resnick 1984; Sternberg 1985; 1986), misconception research in science (Carey 1986), writing (Scardamalia and Bereiter 1985), oral discourse (Delia, O'Keefe, and O'Keefe 1982), and teacher thinking (Berliner 1986, Clark and Peterson 1986).

Recent State Initiatives

Several state education departments have recently legislated new guidelines for curriculum development, instruction, or assessment that represent a radical departure from existing approaches and philosophies. The Michigan State Department of Education and the Michigan State Board of Education (1986), for example, have legislated extensive changes for the Michigan Educational Assessment Program (MEAP) to assess such things as knowledge of the definition of reading as involving an interaction of the reader, the text, and the instructional context; the use of prior knowledge in learning from text; and knowledge of specific reading strategies. This initiative in testing parallels curriculum revisions in reading. Furthermore, Michigan is now in the process of developing a position paper regarding teaching thinking to reflect recent research in cognition and instruction.

Similarly, the Wisconsin Department of Public Instruction (1986) has produced a curriculum guide in reading that explains how the learner constructs meaning by activating prior knowledge and linking the information to be learned to existing knowledge structures or schemata. To implement their guidelines for curriculum objectives, Wisconsin has developed a series of 13 videotapes for staff development and a series of interactive video programs for primary school children called "Story Lords" involving instructional television and computers (Wisconsin Instructional Television 1985).

These states are not alone in their efforts to revise curriculum objectives and instructional materials to reflect recent research from cognitive psychology. The states of California, Florida, Indiana, and Kentucky have passed legislation to change the criteria of textbook adoption (Jones in press). Illinois is in the process of developing a test similar to the new MEAP test, and Connecticut and New Jersey have recently developed tests to assess specific thinking skills (see *Educational Leadership* 1985).

To summarize, there is an increasing consensus among educators and researchers about the goals of learning as defined by cognitive psychology and the implications of these conceptualizations for curriculum, instruction, and assessment. These definitions emphasize the importance of prior knowledge and strategy use in constructing meaning and becoming independent learners.

6

Assumption 2: Learning is Linking New Information to Prior Knowledge.

This assumption emerges from and extends assumptions related to the goals of learning. That is, researchers in various fields believe that information is stored in memory in knowledge structures called schemata. A schema (the singular of schemata) represents the sum of what the individual knows about a given topic or thing. Schemata are not, however, simply collections of information. They are highly interrelated, and they have active properties that allow the learner to engage in a variety of reflective and planful cognitive activities such as making inferences and evaluating (Anderson 1984, Jenkins 1974). For example, existing knowledge structures about socioeconomic class, gangs, and social norms allow the learner to make inferences about the meaning of the title *The Outsiders*, by S. E. Hinton.

Until recently, most of the research on schema theory has been driven by efforts to account for knowledge acquisition in reading (Rumelhart 1980, Spiro 1980). However, schema theory is increasingly becoming a source of our understanding of problem solving, misconceptions in math and science, and listening and writing.

Reading

Schema theorists argue that the model reader usually begins the process of reading by skimming features of the text such as the title, subtitles, graphics, and perhaps small segments of text such as the introduction or summaries. This activates schemata of the content and perhaps schemata of organizational patterns and genre. The reader then uses this information to form hypotheses or predictions about the meaning of the text and the author's intentions. The hypotheses and predictions thus become the purpose for reading in that the reader reads in order to confirm or reject them. At various times, the reader may summarize or compare the new information to existing schemata in terms of their match or fit with the hypotheses, and as the meaning is modified, new questions arise that become the purpose for subsequent reading. Throughout this process, the reader uses prior knowledge to make inferences about the meaning of implicit text (text that is unclear in some way), the relationship among the ideas in a text, the implications of what is read for changing one's prior knowledge, and the application of what is read for understanding phenomena external to the text. (For readable accounts of the process of making hypotheses and inferences from text, see Collins, Brown, and Larkin 1980; Tierney 1983; or Wittrock 1983.)

Problem Solving

The process of linking new information to prior knowledge applies to problem solving as well. In brief, the model learner enters the learning situation with prior knowledge about various categories of problems, content, and a repertoire of existing solutions (Carpenter 1985). That is, he or she may skim the problem features to determine the category of the problem or set of problems (e.g., subtraction, comparison). This process activates prior knowledge of the relevant categories. The activated information is then used to formulate hypotheses about the likely set of procedures for solving the problem and perhaps about estimates regarding the likely outcome or results. As problem solving progresses, the learner makes inferences about the meaning of the problem, especially how to represent it conceptually or graphically. The learner then compares this information to earlier predictions and estimates, revising both prior knowledge of the category and the appropriate procedures or strategy where appropriate. As parts of the problem are solved, new questions arise to guide subsequent learning. Or, as it becomes clear that a given set of procedures is not working, the problem solver may return to prior knowledge to consider alternative strategies, set subgoals, or redefine the problem. (For descriptions of the process of problem solving, see Resnick 1985, Schoenfeld 1985, and Silver 1985, an anthology of papers covering a broad range of topics).

Composing

Interestingly, many of the processes involved in reading are also involved in writing. Long before writing, the writer activates prior knowledge of such things as the topic, specific text structures or writing plans, standards of performance, and audience. Much time may be spent reflecting about how to construct meaning at various levels in terms of the text organization, style, specific phrases or quotes, and so on. As in reading and problem solving, these ideas guide writers to construct tentative productions that they constantly evaluate against prior knowledge, goals, the audience, and so on. Moreover, prior knowledge changes as writers construct new meaning for themselves. (See Flower and Hayes 1981 for a theoretical model of learning; Scardamalia and Berieter 1985 for a comprehensive review; Graves 1978 for descriptions of how students learn to write in school contexts; and Pearson and Tierney 1984 for discussion of parallels in reading and writing.)

Factors Affecting the Use of Prior Knowledge

Not surprisingly, the capability to link new information to prior knowledge is markedly affected by many factors. Generally speaking, students have difficulty activating the appropriate prior knowledge if the information at hand is unclear, disorganized, or somehow lacking in meaning (cf., Bransford and Johnson 1972, Shimmerlik 1978). Purpose in reading also influences what is learned. For example, students told to read a description of a house from the perspective of a home buyer will tend to remember such things as the location and number of bathrooms, whereas students told to read the passage from the perspective of a burglar will be more likely to recall information about security systems and the number and location of windows (Anderson and Pichert 1978).

Other factors that structure the capability to link new information to prior knowledge relate to the characteristics of the learner. Particularly important is the role of domain-specific knowledge. Specifically, lack of information about the topic can seriously constrain the student's capability to recognize patterns, categorize or chunk new information, or generate analogies and related problems/situations (Resnick 1984). A study by de Groot (1965) provides a classic example. He found that chess players had extraordinary recall of the location of chess pieces when they were arranged in meaningful patterns, but no more than average memory when pieces were randomly arranged.

Bransford discusses the problem of *inert knowledge*. This is knowledge that students have but cannot access because they have not linked incoming information with related information and applications or because they lack retrieval strategies (Bransford, Sherwood, Vye, and Rieser 1986). Bransford and his colleagues cite interesting examples of *access failure*. In one experiment, a group of college students was given puzzles along with clues and instructions for using them to solve the puzzle. A second group was given the clues but not the explicit instructions for how to use them. Amazingly, students in the latter group failed to use the clues despite the obvious connections between the clues and the solutions! Other studies of access failure have found that students taught to solve one type of problem may not be able to solve problems that are parallel in structure.

Being able to access and use information is also important in writing. Clearly, the age-old problem of "writer's block" bespeaks of some sort of inert knowledge. Ironically, we can also make the case that "knowledge telling" may stem in part from inert knowledge. Knowledge telling refers to a phenomenon reported by Scardamalia and Bereiter (1985); that is, novice writers often "tell" all they know with little effort to structure the information or develop key ideas, even though they may have a knowledge of organizational patterns that they could use to organize their account.

It is evident from this research that (1) success in many learning situations depends on prior knowledge of specific content, and (2) the existence of prior knowledge is not enough, either for comprehension and recall or for writing and problem solving. Students must be able to access what they know. How do

9

good students do this? Clearly, the learning strategies used to encode, organize, and retrieve information influence how easily knowledge may be accessed, and we will discuss these strategies later. Our focus here is on different types of knowledge.

Types of Knowledge

Researchers describe different types of schemata. Some are content specific, consisting largely of knowledge of concepts and facts, including knowledge of organizational patterns and genre. This type of knowledge is called *declarative knowledge*—the "what" of learning. Other schemata consist of information that tells us how to do something, such as how to predict. This type of knowledge is called *procedural knowledge*—the "how" of learning. Additionally, psychologists refer to knowledge of conditions and contexts associated with specific procedures, often called *conditional knowledge*—the "when" and "why" of learning. Examples include knowing when to skim a text for gist and when to study for in-depth understanding. Other examples include recognizing that two problems are similar and therefore may be solved in similar ways, knowing that it is most efficient to create subgoals, seeing the application of specific concepts, and so on. Compared to novices, experts seem to have relatively more of all three types of knowledge, but researchers increasingly emphasize the importance of conditional knowledge in proficient learning. Moreover, according to Collins, Brown, and Newman (in press), teaching students conditional knowledge is a major component of the most successful instructional programs. (See also Bransford, Sherwood, Vye, Rieser 1986; Paris 1985; Resnick 1984, 1985; Schoenfeld 1985; Winograd and Hare in press).

Assumption 3: Learning is Organizing Knowledge.

Characteristics of Organizational Patterns

An organizational pattern is an identifiable arrangement of ideas or information. An organizational pattern can exist both "inside the head" as knowledge of organizational patterns and "outside the head" as organizational patterns in textual materials. Thus, the compare-and-contrast pattern, for example, can exist in the mind of the learner as well as on paper. The model reader/writer has knowledge of various characteristics of organizational patterns.

Two characteristics of interest here are *genre* and *text structures*. Science fiction, stories, poetry, and documentaries are examples of different genres. Text structures most commonly associated with expository texts are compare and contrast, cause and effect, description, problem and solution, sequential,

10

and concept and examples, according to Anderson and Armbruster (1984). These structures may be found in expository texts across the disciplines and in fiction as well.

Each of these structures has its own distinctive characteristics that skilled readers and writers learn to recognize and use to comprehend and produce information effectively. They know, for example, that authors use *cue words* such as "in contrast" or "once upon a time" to signal a particular type of text structure or genre. Model readers and writers are also aware of key questions or categories of information associated with particular genres, text structures, and content topics. Researchers call these key questions and categories *frames*.

Some frames are generic in that they may be found in various disciplines. Consider the problem/solution text structure. Key questions for such a frame might include the following: Who has the problem? What is the problem? What are the negative effects of the problem? What are possible solutions? What are possible consequences of each solution? Which solution is most appropriate? Slightly different questions may be used as this frame is adapted to particular content areas. Thus, frames are essentially a means of representing text. Frame questions and categories for various text structures that cut across disciplines are given in Planning Guide 1 at the end of this chapter.

Other frames are content specific. Armbruster and Anderson (1985), for example, describe the "region" frame, which includes the following categories of information: surface features, rainfall/weather conditions, products, landmarks, people/culture, and location in relation to other areas. Most geography textbooks cover these categories of information, and it is likely that the skilled reader or writer with knowledge of geography is at least implicitly aware that these categories are typcially found in such texts. Categories for story grammars, such as knowledge about the character's goals and attempts to achieve the goals, are frames typical of narrative texts such as those found in stories and documentaries.

Other examples of content-specific frames may also be found in this book. In Chapter 3, for example, the teacher considers what categories of information are most pertinent to the unit on Jackson. Additionally, Beach, in Chapter 7, discusses how students use literary frames to link new information to prior knowledge. Lindquist, in Chapter 6, refers repeatedly to the need to understand the structure of mathematics and presents various categories of math problems. These catagories are essentially frames for solving story problems, and although much of what is known about the text structures used in prose texts is not applicable to mathematics, this is not becuase the concept of text structures and frames is irrelevant. Rather, the problem is that we are only just beginning to discover how text structures and frames are manifested in the discipline of mathematics; it is hoped that the work of Carpenter (1985) and others in defin-

11

ing math problem categories will make these concepts viable for mathematics educators in future years.

Organizational Patterns in Spoken Language and Graphics

Although most research on organizational patterns has been conducted with students reading or writing prose, we believe that these patterns are fundamental to a wide range of learning tasks inside and outside schools. Consider, for example, a child learning the difference between a dog and a cat, or the student studying types of leaves on a field trip. In both instances, the learner may encode the information as concepts and examples and/or compare-and-contrast patterns. Moreover, these patterns are expressed in spoken language as well as in written texts. The teacher who uses phrases such as "in contrast" or emphasizes the word "because" when speaking is highlighting organizational patterns with specific cue words in much the same way an author signals the use of a particular pattern with signal words. Unlike written language, however, spoken language may also contain body language cues for organizational patterns. Using fingers to indicate sequential patterns or extending an arm with the phrase, "on the one hand," are examples. These parallels between written and spoken language exist because the printed text is essentially a realization of the same language system as the spoken word (Stubbs 1980).

Thus, organizational patterns pervade our thinking, speech, writing, and visual representations of knowledge. How important are organizational patterns in learning in different contexts?

The Effects of Organizational Patterns

In order to answer this question even in general terms, it is important to understand the concept of *considerate* and *inconsiderate text*, coined by Anderson and Armbruster (1984). A text is considerate when the text structure and genre fit the writer's purpose, are well-signaled by cue words, have cohesion and unity of theme, and are audience appropriate in terms of content and vocabulary. Inconsiderate text is text that is difficult to understand because it is poorly organized and poorly written; it may be incoherent, lack signal words, have inappropriate text structures, or have vocabulary that is too dense and inappropriate for the age level. Whether a text is considerate or not has a great deal to do with how the learner comprehends it.

First, considerate text that is well organized and well written may facilitate recall considerably, compared to poorly written text. Numerous studies have shown that students of various ages and proficiency levels tend to use the structural information inherent in a text to organize their recall, if the text is well signaled (e.g., Meyer, Brandt, and Bluth 1980; Meyer 1984). Similarly, students of

12

various ages seem to recall more familiar patterns, such as narratives, better than patterns used in expository information, and more structured patterns, such as compare and contrast, are usually better recalled than open-ended patterns such as description (Amiran and Jones 1982, Raphael and Kirscher 1985, Schnotz 1985). Even very young children are aware of and use the organizational patterns in well-written stories to aid recall (e.g., Stein and Glenn 1979, Bruce 1984).

In contrast, inconsiderate texts are a major reason for comprehension failure. For example, children become confused when elements of story grammars are missing or do not conform to expectations (e.g., Stein and Glenn 1979, Bruce 1984). Moreover, whereas proficient students seem to be able to impose organization and interpretation on poorly organized texts, this is not true of less proficient students. These students respond very poorly to unorganized information, but their performance can be improved markedly by using well-organized passages. The implications of this research suggest that providing well-organized information is especially important for low-achieving students.

These findings are consistent with research on the use of organizational patterns in composition. That is, skilled writers tend to have well-organized and well-signaled written responses when compared to less skilled writers. Skilled writers also have a repertoire of organizational patterns or writing plans, and they use this knowledge to facilitate the various phases of writing (Meyer 1982, 1984; Scardamalia and Bereiter 1985). For example, skilled writers may think about which text structure is most appropriate for their purpose. A major issue in current writing research is to understand the extent to which good writing is the result of domain-specific knowledge versus knowledge of organizational patterns. In all likelihood, both are important.

Additionally, an increasing body of literature on expert/novice research suggests that a key characteristic of experts is having better organized and better integrated knowledge structures than those of novices (e.g., Ballstaedt and Mandl 1985). That is, when experts and novices describe to researchers what they know about a given topic using graphic representations to display what they know, the displays of novices show long strings of concepts that are essentially additive in nature. In contrast, the representations of experts show complex organizational structures with many connections among the parts. Moreover, when experts are asked to learn new information, they integrate and restructure what they learn by changing some concepts and showing how the new concepts relate to old ones. Novices seem simply to add the new information to existing structures in long, unconnected strings. Similar findings have been obtained in a strand of research on expert teachers (e.g., Roehler 1987, Leinhardt 1986). This research is consistent with research on misconceptions (see Anderson, this book). It is also consistent with research in problem solving indicating that experts focus on relating and representing information in a cohesive, verbal, or visual representation of text (see Lindquist, this book).

Finally, there is a growing body of literature on the effects and functions of using frames and graphic outlining on comprehension and recall in training studies. Graphic outlines are visual representations of text such as semantic maps, flow charts, and matrices or two-dimensional tables. While this research is discussed in more detail in Chapter 2, we want to touch on it here since skilled readers and writers appear to be able to use frames and graphic outlines effectively to learn from text and facilitate writing.

Of necessity, we will discuss frames and graphic outlines together throughout this book, since research does not clearly distinguish the effects and functions of one from the other. Holley and Dansereau (1984) refer to learners' use of frames and graphic outlines as spatial learning strategies. Their anthology provides numerous studies that show positive effects on students' comprehension of teaching various systems of graphic outlines, most of which involve some type of frame. Furthermore, several studies suggest that students may be taught to use frames and graphics to structure summaries of information to be learned (e.g., Armbruster, Anderson, and Ostertag 1987; Bean, Singer, Sorter, and Frazee 1986; Darch, Carnine, and Kameenui 1986).

Essentially, skilled readers who have internalized specific frames or graphic structures associated with a particular genre or text structure are able to use that information in various ways: (1) to locate information in what they read, (2) to represent information, (3) to select what is important and unimportant, (4) to impose organization on relatively organized information or information that is only implicitly organized, (5) to integrate and synthesize information from different locations within one text or from various texts, (6) to sequence the order in which information is processed or produced in written responses, (7) to link new information to prior experience, and (8) to restructure prior knowledge.

(Several discussions of organizational patterns focus on classroom applications: Anderson and Armbruster 1984; Armbruster 1986; Jones, Tinzmann, Friedman, and Walker 1987; Van Patten, Chao, and Reigeluth 1986.)

Assumption 4: Learning is Strategic.

What does it mean to say that learning is strategic? In this section, we discuss the metacognitive aspects of being strategic and the operating characteristics of skilled learning. A discussion of specific strategies and skills will be deferred until the next section because different strategies are used in different phases of learning. Here we will simply point out that a skill is a mental activity that can be applied to specific learning tasks. Predicting, summarizing, and mapping are examples of skills. Strategies are specific procedures or ways of executing a given skill. Using a specific set of summarizing rules or a particular procedure for predicting are examples of strategies.

Metacognitive Aspects of Learning

Learning is strategic in that model learners are aware of and control their efforts to use particular skills and strategies. These characteristics of learning are well defined in the concepts of *strategic learning*, coined by Paris, Lipson, and Wixson (1983), and the *good strategy user*, coined by Pressley, Borkowski, and Schneider (in press).

Awareness refers not only to knowledge of specific cognitive strategies but also to knowledge of how to use them and when they should be used. Control refers, in part, to the capability to monitor and direct the success of the task at hand, such as recognizing that comprehension has failed, using fix-up strategies, and checking an obtained answer against an estimation. Additionally, a large part of controlling strategy use relates to learners' perseverance in motivating themselves, in making decisions about the importance of the task, in managing their time, and in their attribution of success or failure (Paris and Winograd in progress). That is, good learners tend to stick to the job or task until it is done to their satisfaction and to attribute their success to their own efforts. They are aware that they can do a great deal to control their own learning, and they constantly work to select appropriate strategies and to monitor strategy use throughout the learning process. Thus, good strategy users learn how to learn independently and efficiently. In contrast, low-achieving students tend to attribute the causes of their performance to luck or other factors beyond their control and therefore are less involved in planning, monitoring, and revising.

Characteristics of Skills and Strategies

Because of the vast literature on skills and strategies, we limit ourselves here to a few summary statements of some themes of recent research. (See Endnote 1 for references to this literature by subject area).

1. Effective learning involves being able to access particular strategies with flexibility. Thus, an effective learner or good strategy user knows when to use a given strategy as well as when to abandon it and select another one.

2. Expert learners appear to be able to develop a repertoire of effective cognitive and metacognitive learning strategies spontaneously while progressing through school, that is, without specially designed interventions.

3. The behavior of younger and low-achieving students can sometimes be

substantially modified by effective interventions involving explicit strategy instruction and appropriate learning contexts.

4. There is no evidence in the research literature for limiting instruction for less proficient or younger students to instruction in basic skills. To the contrary, both types of students are able to learn what has been called "higher-order thinking skills" and strategies when provided with effective instruction.

5. Substantial evidence indicates that many skills and strategies do not transfer, sometimes not even to similar tasks. In general, the more specific the skill or strategy, the less likely it is to transfer. On the other hand, the more general the strategy, the less useful it is. In teaching students to use any skill, it is important to teach students how to transfer the skill or strategy to various tasks.

6. Many of the same skills are critical across various content areas. While no single list of skills exists that is applicable to all content areas, a number of core skills seem to show up in the research literature in various subject areas. Examples of core skills include activating prior knowledge, representing the text or problem, monitoring one's progress, and summarizing.

7. There is a strong belief in the research literature that learning is fragmented by isolated skills instruction, specifically when skills are broken down into myriads of smaller skills and taught as ends in themselves. This does not mean that skills instruction should be abandoned. To the contrary, there is a need for explicit instruction in particular skills, and in some cases subskills. And there is some agreement that students learn best when skills instruction progresses from being teacher directed with a strong emphasis on modeling and guided practice to being student directed, involving independent learning. How this should be done is still controversial.

Limited Cognitive Capacity and the Thinking Skills Controversy

Basically, there are two points of view in this controversy. On the one hand, developers of thinking skills programs and some other researchers tend to argue that skills should be taught explicitly in adjunct courses, so that learning of skills does not interfere with learning of content. On the other hand, some researchers believe that students will acquire learning and thinking strategies in the course of learning content and concepts in specific content areas, so that explicit skills instruction is not required or, if it is, it should be given within the context of content courses (e.g., Glaser 1985). This controversy involves many complex issues, but we will limit ourselves to three.

The first issue is related to the notion of *general versus specific skills*. Those who advocate explicit skills instruction believe that it is useful to teach students general skills that apply to various types of problems and situations. Others believe that the ability to make inferences and to generate new information depends on content-specific information and that these strategies do not transfer—therefore, there is little point in providing explicit skills instruction (see Bransford, Sherwood, Vye, and Rieser 1986; Campione and Armbruster 1985).

A second argument relates to the concept of *limited cognitive capacity*. Mandler (1967) and others have shown that learners' capability to hold items of information in working memory is limited to five to nine discrete items. If substantial amounts of that capacity are used for skills instruction, less processing "space" is left over for content instruction. Therefore, since content is most important, we should not consume that space with skills instruction (Kamil, personal communication, 1986). Ironically, Feuerstein (1980) uses this same concept to argue for separate skills instruction. According to him, less proficient students especially need substantial instruction in skills that are prerequisite to effective thinking in the content areas. Therefore, we should not confound the learning situation by trying to teach skills and content at the same time.

Third, an issue closely related to this debate is the issue of *how to sequence skills instruction*. Clearly, if an instructor is teaching skills in an adjunct skills course, it is useful to sequence the instruction from simple to complex. However, the question arises as to the extent to which students need instruction in prerequisite subskills. A widespread practice in schools is to break each skill into skill hierarchies such that the learner must master "lower level" skills before attempting "higher level" skills. While everyone recognizes that these procedures are essential for concepts and skills that are in fact hierarchical, such as learning addition before multiplication, there is a danger that this practice will fractionate learning in instances where holistic understanding is desirable, as in reading (Anderson et al. 1985). In such instances, it may be possible to teach given skills holistically but with increasing complexity and diversity of content (Burton, Brown, and Fischer 1984; Collins, Brown, and Newman in press; Lesgold 1986). Whatever the context, it may be helpful to sequence instructional strategies to provide modeling, coaching, and the like (Collins, Brown, and Newman in press).

Our position is consistent with that of Campione and Armbruster (1985). They indicate that less proficient students may need sustained explicit skills instruction with lots of practice and feedback. Yet they acknowledge that such instruction would interfere with content instruction if content and sustained skills instruction were given simultaneously. We would therefore support adjunct skills instruction with a strong content emphasis and much effort to make applications to the content areas, but only for younger and low-achieving students. For other students, we believe there is much merit to teaching skills within the context of content courses, where possible.

Assumption 5:
Learning Occurs in Phases Yet Is Recursive.

The new research also emphasizes that reading, writing, and problem solving are complex thinking processes involving different skills and strategies at different phases of learning. Although researchers differ in the extent to which they delineate specific phases and in the labels they use to describe the phases, we argue that thinking generally occurs in three phases: preparing for learning, on-line processing, and consolidating/extending. This view of thinking and learning as having three phases is consistent with other models (see Endnote 2). We will show how these phases apply to reading and then consider parallel processes in other areas.

Preparing for Learning

Initially, the model reader does something to activate prior knowledge. Sometimes this might entail skimming the text, a set of problems, or possibly a data base. At other times, this activating activity might be a mental review or summary of previous learnings. The function of these activities is to focus attention on the content, text features, and appropriate reading strategies (Mayer 1984). The learner may use this information to form predictions, questions, or hypotheses about the meaning of the specific text at hand. It is also during this phase that the learner may set specific purposes for reading, such as answering specific questions, testing hypotheses, or confirming predictions.

On-line Processing

As reading progresses, hypotheses are assessed against information in the text or prior knowledge. Sometimes hypotheses are confirmed and new ideas are assimilated. At other times, hypotheses are rejected because they are not supported, or judgment is withheld because of inadequate information. As new ideas are assimilated or held in abeyance, readers raise new questions that form the basis for new predictions and hypotheses. Thus, learning is essentially a start/pause process in which readers monitor their comprehension by skills such as self-questioning, looking back to verify or clarify, looking ahead to anticipate, selecting and summarizing what is important, and comparing new information to prior knowledge. In this phase, the reader is working actively to integrate incoming information with knowledge structures that have just been reactivated. In essence, readers organize what they read and generate meaning as they link individual bits of information to each other and to prior knowledge.

Consolidating/Extending

After reading various text segments and forming some sense of their meaning, readers may engage in a variety of activities to understand the text as a whole, to consolidate what was learned, and to integrate new constructions with prior knowledge in long-term memory. Some of these cognitive activities, such as summarizing and linking new information to prior knowledge, may be the same as those engaged in during on-line processing. Others involve connecting ideas from different parts of the text using categorizing, mapping or graphic outlining, looking back to identify gaps in understanding, and the like. In the case of misconceptions or contradictory information, the model reader will probably spend some time trying to reconcile the disciplinary view with naive assumptions based on intuition or incomplete observation stored in long-term memory. Still other consolidating activities involve efforts to articulate what was learned about the content or the use of a given strategy. Additionally, the model reader may seek to extend what was learned by applying the new knowledge or skills to novel examples and thinking about how to transfer what was learned. Schoenfeld (1985) refers to such considerations as "debriefing" sessions.

Recursive and Nonlinear Thinking

Unlike writing researchers and thinking researchers, few reading researchers refer explicitly to reading as a nonlinear thinking process. An exception here is Vygotsky (1962), who states that when we connect a new idea to something familiar, we may have to go back into memory and verify it or else connect it to something different and rethink. These processes recur. Although the concept of recursiveness is not prominent in reading research, this notion of recurring cycles of thought is strongly implied in most accounts of reading as well as in rationales for instruction involving the start/pause process described above. That is, anticipating what is to come and thinking back to compare new information to prior knowledge within each phase of reading are fundamentally nonlinear thinking strategies. Similarly, the cycles of stopping to check for understanding or reflect on the author's purpose, looking back to clarify or verify and the like are inherently nonlinear in nature and involve nonlinear reading (not reading word by word or line by line).

Phases of Learning in Other Areas

While there are different delineations and labels for the phases of learning in composing, listening, and speaking, (as there are in reading research), proficient learners engage different skills and strategies in different phases of thinking as they compose, listen, generate arguments, and engage in other thinking activities. Models of listening (e.g., Lundsteen 1979) and argumentation (e.g., Toulmin 1984), for example, conceptualize information processing in terms of flowcharts with branching procedures, allowing for nonlinear thinking and sometimes iterative cycles. Similarly, models of writing (e.g., Flower and Hayes 1981) emphasize that the process of writing consists largely of iterative cycles of planning, drafting, monitoring, editing, and revising, including the possibility of returning to the planning stages and replanning the whole composition. Thus, as in accounts of reading, these descriptions of writing suggest that writing is sequential yet has recursive cycles.

Although there is little explicit reference in writing, listening, and argumentation research to consolidating and extending learning, it is evident that model learners refine and restructure their knowledge in the process of writing, developing an argument, and listening. To the extent that this is true, it seems likely that articulating new learnings and questions in conferences, peer editing, and self-questioning would be important activities to consolidate and extend learning. These notions of process are compatible with the description of phases of learning in reading research described above.

The literature also has references to phases of problem solving. No doubt much of this stems from Polya's (1945) model identifying four phases: understanding the problem, devising a plan, carrying out the plan, and looking back to check for errors as well as to determine general principles and their applications. Lester (1985) has modified Polya's model to emphasize the coordination of metacognitive and cognitive strategies before problem solving (orientation), during problem solving (organization and execution), and after it (verification). While these models seem somewhat linear and sequential, verification refers to evaluating in every phase in much the same way that is suggested in reading research. Moreover, there is reference to nonlinear thinking in problem solving (Resnick 1984, Schoenfeld 1985). That is, problem solving is not merely a matter of deciding what strategies to use, applying them in a specific order, and finding a solution; there is much experimentation, reflection, rethinking, and seeking alternative solutions.

Finally, conceptual change in science also seems to occur in phases. That is, the science learner apparently has a broad range of misconceptions about light, motion, photosynthesis, and other physical phenomena. These views conflict with disciplinary knowledge but are rarely confronted directly. Skilled learners may be aware early on that the new information contradicts or is inconsistent with prior knowledge. Thus, they seek first to understand the new information as they process the information (building) and then to reconcile it with the old information (consolidation). Learners who do not progress through this process of confrontation and integration may maintain contradictory or inconsistent views or have incomplete understanding.

Planning Guide 1 at the end of this chapter attempts to capture the essence of these phases of conceptual change for various thinking processes. This guide should not be seen as a checklist of skills to be taught as ends in themselves. Nor should it be thought that any one sequence of learning contains all of these skills, or that a skill listed in one phase is likely to be used only in that phase. Rather, the skills in this guide represent a repertoire of selected skills that the learner may call on at any given time to aid learning in a particular situation. Possibly, all or most of these skills might be used in some learning situations, just as it is possible that only a few of them may be called upon for a particular task. And certainly, given the recursive nature of learning and thinking, it is likely that the same skill may be used in more than one phase. The skills are organized in phases because learning seems to occur in phases, and different strategies may be used in each phase (cf. Marzano, Brandt, Hughes, Jones, Presseisen, Rankin, and Suhor in press).

Assumption 6: Learning is Influenced by Development.

An important strand of recent research involves comparisons of experts and skilled learners versus novices and less proficient students as well as comparisons of younger and older students. Although many differences among these groups have been documented, most of them relate to differences in prior knowledge, including knowledge of vocabulary, and to differences in the repertoire of cognitive and metacognitive strategies. Hence, it is not clear whether skilled students, compared to unskilled students, begin school with greater prior knowledge and more effective strategies or whether these differences develop over time. Probably both situations are true and it is evident that, once established, these differences tend to be self-perpetuating without intervention.

Less Proficient Students

Fortunately, substantial evidence indicates that low-achieving students can be taught to use various learning/thinking strategies such as categorizing or summarizing (e.g., Brown, Campione, and Day 1981; Holley and Dansereau 1984; Weinstein and Underwood 1985). At the same time, low-achieving students need diverse opportunities to practice and apply skills to varied contexts with corrective feedback as well as sustained, explicit strategy instruction with strong metacognitive components (Garner, Hare, Alexander, Haynes, and Winograd 1984). In fact, Derry and Murphy (1986) state that we know how to teach

21

the learner to use learning strategies, but that is not enough if the metacognitive processes are not operating effectively.

Automaticity

Automaticity is the capability of the learner to think quickly with little awareness of processing information consciously. It is a major issue concerning the development of expertise in acquiring knowledge of content and the development of skill proficiency. That is, several strands of developmental research in reading and learning indicate that proficient learners process information much more quickly than do less proficient learners (e.g, Lesgold 1986). Furthermore, proficient learners may not benefit from strategy training (Pressley et al. in press). Instead, explicit strategy instruction may even inhibit model learners' performance of a variety of learning and reading tasks. Generally, this research suggests that proficient learning involves a certain degree of automaticity that may be disrupted by inappropriate interventions.

*   *   *

In summary, we found that thinking is oriented toward general purposes: to understand, to construct meaning, to solve problems, to become independent as learners. The essence of learning, according to various strands of research, is to link new information to prior knowledge. Good learners do this by drawing upon a repertoire of cognitive and metacognitive strategies. It was argued that these strategies could be learned in various sequences. Knowledge refers not only to knowledge of the facts and concepts related to specific topic areas, but also to knowledge of cognitive and metacognitive strategies and knowledge of the genres and organizational patterns used in different types of text.

Additionally, thinking is a process that typically involves anticipation; online processing that builds on what is learned; and consolidating, integrating, and extending. However, a key part of this argument is that thinking is neither continuous nor linear. That is, the model learner may stop thinking at any time to reflect on the process of learning, the relationship among ideas and information in different parts of a text or data base, or the linkages between new information and prior knowledge. Additionally, the learner may return to earlier hypotheses to confirm or reject them as well as test incoming information against previously held standards of logic or prior knowledge. In fact, the learner may use sets of strategies in variable sequences or in iterative cycles.

In closing, we might describe learning with an analogy to a well-orchestrated symphony, aimed to blend both familiar and new sounds. A symphony is the complex interplay of composer, conductor, the repertoire of instruments, and the various dimensions of music. Each instrument is used strategically to interact with other instruments toward a rich construction of themes progressing in phases, with some themes recurring and others driving the movement forward toward a conclusion or resolution. Finally, each symphony stands alone in its meaning, yet has a relationship to the symphonies that came before and those that will come later. Similarly, learning is a complex interaction of the learner, the instructional materials, the repertoire of available learning strategies, and the context, including the teacher. The skilled learner approaches each task strategically toward the goal of constructing meaning. Some strategies focus on understanding the incoming information, others strive to relate the meaning to earlier predictions, and still others work to integrate the new information with prior knowledge.

Planning Guide 1
Frames for Generic Organizational Patterns

TEXTS CONTAINING ONLY ONE MAJOR ELEMENT OR IDEA AND SUPPORTING INFORMATION

1. **Description of One Thing.** Description of one thing in literature may focus on the characters, places, and objects. In such descriptions, it is critical to identify the thing being described and its attributes. Descriptive texts are sometimes referred to as list or collection structures because the attributes may be described in any order. Description in context area passages may be guided by content-specific frames such as the region frame.

2. **Proposition/Support.** Proposition/support is a very common paragraph structure. In its most simple form, it is a statement plus information supporting the statement. These structures are difficult to recognize because there are few easily recognizable signal words. Moreover, close inspection often reveals that they are other patterns such as description, or concept/definition. Frame categories for a theme paragraph include the statement of the theme, elaboration and interpretation of the theme, and supporting information such as examples, quotes, and other information. Proposition/support paragraphs often have more than one level of ideas, such as major and minor ideas.

3. **Argumentation for a Single Thing.** These frames also provide for varying degrees of complexity. Simple arguments contain only two categories of information: the statement of a conclusion (an opinion or action) and premises (reasons, examples, facts, quotes, etc.) which support the conclusion. More complex argumentation frames have explanations for the reasons and complex chains of reasoning as well as support for the reasons. What is critical in comprehending and composing an argument is the adequacy of the logic linking the premises to the conclusion. This logic includes questioning the adequacy of the information in many instances but focuses on the quality of reasoning.

4. **Concept/Definition for One Thing.** To understand a single concept, it is important to know the following: What is the thing? What category does it belong to? What are its critical attributes? Other questions may include: How does it work? What does it do? What are its functions? What are examples of it? And, where appropriate, what are some nonexamples? Concept/definition paragraphs arise in literature in such works as *The Search for Excellence* by Thomas Peters and Robert Waterman, or *Crime and Punishment* by Fydor Dostoevski.

TEXTS DESCRIBING A SEQUENCE

5. **Sequential Texts.** Sequential structures involve either a chronological order or logical order, even if they are not presented in the correct order. Therefore, it is often an important task to understand or predict the correct *sequence of events*. In literature and historical texts, this may mean integrating the events in

flashbacks or forecasts of events to come. In content texts, sequential texts may be *steps in a procedure* (e.g., how milk is pasteurized), *stages of development of something* (e.g., the stages in the life cycle of primates).

In such instances, it is important for the teacher and students to address the following categories: identify the name of the object, procedure, or initiating event; describe the stages, steps, series, showing how one leads to another; and describe the final outcome.

6. **Goal/Action/Outcome.** Since much of human behavior in literature or any narrative is goal oriented (e.g., winning out when one is handicapped, surviving under difficult circumstances), a useful way to summarize such behavior is to identify the goals, actions, and outcomes of the person or group. Clearly, there is a sequential component in goal/action/outcome frames, though it is often the case that the goal is not revealed or implied early in the text.

TEXTS CONTAINING TWO OR MORE IMPORTANT ELEMENTS/IDEAS

7. **Compare/Contrast Two or More Things.** The two elements in a compare/contrast frame are the set of similarities and the set of differences. Typically, these structures identify what is being compared, the points that are being compared, the ways in which they are similar, the ways in which they are different, and sometimes a summary statement indicating that the things compared are more alike than different or vice versa. However, there are different ways to organize compare/contrast structures: the whole set of similarities followed by the whole set of differences or vica versa; point by point comparisons of the similarities and differences; and mixes of these two patterns.

Descriptions of two or more things and discussion of two or more concepts or a concept hierarchy involve all of the categories of compare/contrast frames.

8. **Problem/Solution.** Most problem-solving frames pertaining to people in fiction and history focus on identifying who had the problem, the general definition of the problem, its causes and effects, actions taken to solve the problem, and the effects of the actions. Such frames may also contain elements of decision making such as defining the available options, resources, and the consequences of each option. Problem/ solution frames for literature may focus on identifying the process of looking for solutions and the causal connection or explanation for the solution. Problem/solution frames also have a sequential component.

9. **Cause/Effect.** These frames involve establishing the effect, its cause or causes, and often an explanation linking the cause(s) to the effect. Complex cause/effect frames may involve a sequential chain of causes and/or interaction of various factors as well as multiple effects. Clearly, these frames are inherently sequential in reality, though descriptions often begin with the effects and then discuss the causes.

10. **Interaction Frames (Cooperation and Conflict).** Much of good literature involves the interaction of two or more persons or groups (e.g., the interaction of a child and an animal or a child and his/her parents). To comprehend the nature of their interaction, the key questions are: What are the persons/groups? What were their goals? What was the nature of their interaction: conflict or cooperation? How did they act and react? (Did the interaction involve conflict or cooperation?) What was the outcome for each person/ group? Interaction frames contain both sequential organization and compare/contrast organization. This pattern is present in William Golding's *Lord of the Flies* at two different levels. One level is the interaction of the main characters, and another level is the conflict between the democratic group and the totalitarian group.

Reprinted with permission from *Thinking Skills Instruction in English/Language Arts*, published by the National Education Association, 1987.

Planning Guide 2
Thinking Processes

Thinking Processes	Instructional Strategies
PREPARATION FOR LEARNING	PREPARATION FOR LEARNING

Comprehend objective/task
define learning objectives
consider task/audience
determine criteria for success

Preview/Select materials/cues at hand
skim features, graphic aids
determine content focus/organizational pattern

Activate prior knowledge
access content and vocabulary
access categories and structure
access strategies/plans

Focus interest/Set purpose
form hypotheses and questions/make predictions
represent/organize ideas (categorize/outline)

ON-LINE PROCESSING (Text Segments) — PRESENTATION OF CONTENT

Modify Hypotheses/Clarify ideas
check hypotheses, predictions, questions
compare to prior knowledge
ask clarification questions
examine logic of argument, flow of ideas
generate new questions

Integrate ideas
select important concepts/words
connect and organize ideas, summarize

Assimilate new ideas
articulate changes in knowledge
evaluate ideas/products
withhold judgment

CONSOLIDATING/EXTENDING ("The Big Picture") — APPLICATION AND INTEGRATION

Integrate/organize meaning for whole
categorize and integrate information, conclude
summarize key ideas and connections
evaluate/revise/edit

Assess achievement of purpose/learning
compare new learnings to prior knowledge
identify gaps in learning and information
generate new questions/next steps

Extend learning
translate/apply to new situations
rehearse and study

Adapted from *Thinking Skills Instruction in English/Language Arts*, Copyright © 1987. National Education Association.

Endnotes

[1] *For Strategies for Comprehending Written and Spoken Prose:* See Anderson and Armbruster (1984) for a good discussion of research on study skills; Collins, Brown, and Larkin (1980) for a description of the skills used in making inferences from text; Derry and Murphy (1986) for a comprehensive review of research on learning strategies and issues about implementing them in the classroom; Jonasen (1985) for a review of research on strategies that utilize the various features of a text; Friedman (1983), O'Keefe (1986), and Lundsteen (1979) for discussions of critical thinking skills involved in listening; Mayer (1984) and Weinstein and Mayer (1985) for a good discussion of elaboration strategies in which the learner focuses on constructing linkages among the ideas to prior knowledge and to each other through analogies and other elaboration techniques. See also Weinstein and Underwood (1985) for a discussion of an effective learning strategies course and a test for assessing the use of specific learning strategies.

For Composing Prose Text and Argumentation: See Applebee (1984) for a discussion of writing and reasoning; Delia, O'Keefe, and O'Keefe (1982) and La Fleur (1985) for descriptions of the strategies and skills involved in argumentation and oral discourse; Scardamalia and Berieter (1985) for a comprehensive review of the range of skills and strategies involved in writing.

For Problem-Solving Skills and Strategies: See Branca (1985) for a description of skills involved in problem formulation, problem solving, verifying, and integrating; Bransford, Sherwood, Vye, and Rieser (1986) and Gick (1986) for a discussion of the relation between domain specific knowledge and skills knowledge and the problem of transfer; Roth (1985) for in-depth descriptions of the effective and ineffective strategies middle school students use in processing science texts and dealing with misconceptions; Schoenfeld (1985) and Thompson (1985) for extensive descriptions of the strategies and skills needed for problem solving in mathematics; and Mayer (1985) for the implications of cognitive psychology on learning and instruction for mathematical problem solving.

For General Classifications of Thinking Skills: See Costa (1985a) for a comprehensive anthology of program developers and analysts of the thinking skills movement; Segal, Chipman, and Glaser (1985) for descriptions and analysis of exemplary thinking skills programs and issues related to implementing and evaluating them; Chance (1986) and Nickerson, Perkins, and Smith (1985) for recent descriptions and classifications of thinking skills programs; Marzano, Brandt, Hughes, Jones, Presseisen, Rankin, and Suhor (in press) for a comprehensive and systematic treatment of the thinking skills/strategies and processes involved in the various dimensions of thinking; and Baron and Sternberg (1987) for an excellent discussion of issues and themes in the thinking skills movement and the presentation of selected programs.

For Metacognitive Strategies: See Brown (1985) for a discussion of teaching reading as (metacognitive) thinking and the implications for curriculum and instruction; and Brown, Bransford, Ferrara, and Campione (1983) for a general statement of the role of metacognition. See Palincsar and Brown (1984); Paris, Cross, and Wixson (1983); Pressley, Borkowski, and Schneider (in press); and Bean, Singer, Sorter, and Frazee (1986) for descriptions of effective training programs with a strong metacognitive component. See also Thomas and Rohwer (1986) for a discussion of a model of autonomous learning in contexts requiring academic studying.

[2] The notion that learning progresses in phases is hardly a new idea. It is new in comparison to the traditional stimulus-response model of behaviorism. However, Costa

(1985b) compared 16 different models of thinking and found that all of them conceptualized instruction in terms of three phases, albeit using very different terminology. Basically, most of these models follow an input/organization/output model that is prominent in current information processing models.

References

Amiran, M. R., and B. F. Jones. "Toward a New Definition of Readability." *Educational Psychologist* 17 (1982): 13-30.

Anderson, R. C. "Role of Reader's Schema in Comprehension, Learning and Memory." In *Learning to Read in American Schools: Basal Readers and Content Texts*, edited by R. C. Anderson, J. Osborn, and R. J. Tierney. Hillsdale, N.J.: Erlbaum, 1984.

Anderson, R. C., E. H. Hiebert, J. A. Scott, and I. A. G. Wilkinson. *Becoming a Nation of Readers: The Report of the Commission on Reading.* Urbana, Ill.: University of Illinois, 1985.

Anderson, R., and J. Pichert. "Recall of Previously Unrecallable Information Following a Shift in Perspective." *Journal of Verbal Learning and Verbal Behavior* 17 (1978): 1-12.

Anderson, T. H., and B. B. Armbruster. "Content Area Textbooks." In *Learning to Read in American Schools: Basal Readers and Content Texts*, edited by R. C. Anderson, J. Osborn, and R. J. Tierney. Hillsdale, N.J.: Erlbaum, 1984.

Applebee, A. N. "Writing and Reasoning." *Review of Educational Research* 54 (1984): 577-596.

Armbruster, B. B. "Schema Theory and Design of Instructional Text." *Educational Psychologist* 51 (1986): 11.

Armbruster, B. B., and T. H. Anderson. "Frames: Structure for Informational Texts." In *Technology of Text, Vol. 2*, edited by D. H. Jonassen. Englewood Cliffs, N.J.: Educational Technology Publications, 1985.

Armbruster, B. B., T. H. Anderson, and J. Ostertag. "Does Text Structure/Summarization Facilitate Learning from Text?" *Reading Research Quarterly* 22 (1987).

Ballstaedt, S. P., and H. Mandl. *Diagnosis of Knowledge Structures in Text Learning* (Technical Report No. 37). Tubingen, West Germany: Deutsches Institut fur Fernstudien an der Universitat Tubingen, 1985.

Baron, J. B., and R. J. Sternberg. *Teaching Thinking Skills: Theory and Practice.* New York: W. H. Freeman, 1987.

Bean, T. W., H. Singer, J. Sorter, and C. Frazee. "The Effect of Metacognition Instruction in Outlining and Graphic Organizer Construction on Students' Comprehension in a Tenth-Grade World History Class." *Journal of Reading Behavior* 18 (1983): 153-170.

Berliner, D. C. "In Pursuit of the Expert Pedagogue." *Educational Researcher* 15 (April 1986): 5-14.

Branca, N. A. "Mathematical Problem Solving: Lessons from the British Experience." In *Teaching and Learning Mathematical Problem Solving*, edited by E. A. Silver. Hillsdale, N.J.: Erlbaum, 1985.

Bransford, J. D., and M. K. Johnson. "Contextual Prerequisites of Comprehension and Recall." *Journal of Verbal Learning and Verbal Behavior* 11 (1972): 717-726.

Bransford, J. D., R. Sherwood, N. Vye, and J. Rieser. "Teaching Thinking and Problem Solving." *American Psychologist* 41 (1986): 1078-1089.

Brown, A. L. "Metacognitive Development and Reading." In *Theoretical Issues in Read-*

ing Comprehension, edited by R. J. Spiro, B. C. Bruce, and W. F. Brewer. Hillsdale, N.J.: Erlbaum, 1980.

Brown, A. L. *Teaching Students to Think as They Read: Implications for Curriculum Reform* (Reading Education Rep. No. 58). Urbana: University of Illinois, The Center for the Study of Reading, 1985.

Brown, A. L., J. D. Bransford, R. A. Ferrara, and J. C. Campione. "Learning, Remembering, and Understanding." In *Handbook of Child Psychology, Vol. 3*, edited by J. H. Flavell and E. M. Markham. New York: Wiley, 1983.

Brown, A. L., J. C. Campione, and J. Day. "Learning to Learn: On Training Students to Learn from Texts." *Educational Researcher* 10 (April 1981): 14-24.

Bruce, B. "A New Point of View on Children's Stories." In *Learning to Read in American Schools: Basal Readers and Content Texts*, edited by R. C. Anderson, J. Osborn, and R. J. Tierney. Hillsdale, N.J.: Erlbaum, 1984.

Burns, M. "Teaching 'What To Do' in Arithmetic vs. Teaching 'What to Do and Why.'" *Educational Leadership* 43 (April 1986): 34-38.

Burton, R., J. S. Brown, and G. Fischer. "Skiing as a Model of Instruction." In *Everyday Cognition: Its Development in Social Context*, edited by B. Rogoff and J. Lave. Cambridge: Harvard University, 1984.

Campione, J. C., and B. B. Armbruster. "Acquiring Information from Texts: An Analysis of Four Approaches." In *Thinking and Learning Skills: Relating Instruction to Research, Vol. 1*, edited by J. W. Segal, S. F. Chipman, and R. Glaser. Hillsdale, N.J.: Erlbaum, 1985.

Carey, S. "Cognitive Science and Science Education." *American Psychologist* 41 (1986): 1123-1130.

Carpenter, T. P. "Learning to Add and Subtract: An Exercise in Problem Solving." In *Teaching and Learning Mathematical Problem Solving*, edited by E. A. Silver. Hillsdale, N.J.: Erlbaum, 1985.

Chance, P. *Thinking in the Classroom*. New York: Teachers College Press, 1986, pp. 101-107.

Clark, C. M., and P. L. Peterson. "Teachers' Thought Processes." In *Handbook of Research on Teaching*, edited by M. C. Wittrock. New York: Macmillan, 1986.

Collins, A., J. S. Brown, and S. Newman. "Cognitive Apprenticeship: Teaching Students the Craft of Reading, Writing, and Mathematics." In *Cognition and Instruction: Issues and Agendas*, edited by L. B. Resnick. Hillsdale, N.J.: Erlbaum, in press.

Collins, A., J. S. Brown, and K. M. Larkin. "Inference in Text Understanding." In *Theoretical Issues in Reading Comprehension*, edited by R. J. Spiro, B. C. Bruce, and W. F. Brewer. Hillsdale, N.J.: Erlbaum, 1980.

Costa, A. L., ed. *Developing Minds: A Resource Book for Teaching Thinking*. Alexandria, Va.: Association for Supervision and Curriculum Development, 1985a.

Costa, A. L. "Toward a Model of Human Intellectual Functioning." In *Developing Minds: A Resource Book for Teaching Thinking*, edited by A. L. Costa. Alexandria, Va.: Association for Supervision and Curriculum Development, 1985b.

de Groot, A. *Thought and Choice in Chess*. The Hague: Mouton and Company, 1965.

Delia, J. G., B. J. O'Keefe, and D. J. O'Keefe. "The Constructist Approach to Communication." In *Human Communication Theory*, edited by F. E. X. Dance. New York: Harper & Row, 1982.

Derry, S. J., and D. A. Murphy. "Designing Systems That Train Learning Ability: From Theory to Practice." *Review of Educational Research* 56 (1986): 1-39.

28

Durkin, D. "What Classroom Observations Reveal About Reading Comprehension Instruction." *Reading Research Quarterly* 15 (1978-79): 481-533.

Edmonds, R. R. "Programs of School Improvement: An Overview." *Educational Leadership* 40 (December 1982): 4-11.

Educational Leadership. Theme issue: "The Search for Solutions to the Testing Problem." 42 (April 1985).

Feuerstein, R. *Instrumental Enrichment.* Baltimore: University Park Press, 1980.

Flower, L., and J. R. Hayes. "The Pregnant Pause: An Enquiry into the Nature of Planning." *Research in the Teaching of English* 15 (1981): 229-244.

Friedman, P. *Listening Processes: Attention, Understanding, Evaluation.* Washington, D.C.: National Education Association.

Garner, R., V. C. Hare, P. Alexander, J. Haynes, and P. N. Winograd. "Inducing Use of a Text Lookback Strategy Among Unsuccessful Readers." *American Educational Research Journal* 21 (1984): 789-798.

Gick, M. L. "Problem-Solving Strategies." *Educational Psychologist* 21 (1986): 99-120.

Glaser, R. "Learning and Instruction: A Letter for a Time Capsule." In *Thinking and Learning Skills, Vol. 2,* edited by S. F. Chipman, J. W. Segal, and R. Glaser. Hillsdale, N.J.: Erlbaum, 1985.

Graves, D. H. *Balance the Basics: Let Them Write.* New York: The Ford Foundation, 1978.

Holley, C. D., and D. F. Dansereau. *Spatial Learning Strategies: Techniques, Applications, and Related Issues.* New York: Academic Press, 1984.

Hunt, J. M. *Human Intelligence.* New Brunswick, N.J.: Dutton, 1972.

Jenkins, J. "Remember That Old Theory of Memory? Well, Forget It!" *American Psychologist* 29 (1974): 785-795.

Jensen, A. R. "How Much Can We Boost IQ and Scholastic Achievement?" *Harvard Educational Review* 39 (1969): 1-124.

Jonasen, D. H. "Generative Learning vs. Mathemagenic Control of Text Processing." In *The Technology of Text, Vol. 2,* edited by D. H. Jonassen. Englewood Cliffs, N.J.: Educational Technology Press, 1985.

Jones, B. F. "Text Learning Strategy Instruction: Guidelines from Theory to Practice." In *Learning and Study Strategy Research: Issues in Assessment, Instruction, and Evaluation,* edited by E. Goetz, P. Alexander, and C. E. Weinstein. New York: Academic Press, in press.

Jones, B. F., M. Tinzmann, L. B. Friedman, and B. J. Walker. *Teaching Thinking Skills in English/Language Arts.* Washington, D.C.: National Education Association, 1987.

LaFleur, G. B. "A New Look at Meaning in Systems to Argument." In *Argument and Social Practice: Proceedings of the Fourth SCA/AFA Conference on Argumentation,* edited by J. R. Cox, M. O. Sillars, and G. B. Walker. Washington, D.C.: Speech Communication Association, 1985.

Leinhardt, G. "Expertise in Mathematics Teaching." *Educational Leadership* 43 (1986): 23-27.

Lesgold, A. M. "Producing Automatic Performance." Paper presented at the annual meeting of the American Educational Research Association, San Francisco, April 1986.

Lester, F. K. "Methodological Considerations in Research in Mathematical Problem Solving Instruction." In *Teaching and Learning Mathematical Problem Solving,* edited by E. A. Silver. Hillsdale, N.J.: Erlbaum, 1985.

Lundsteen, S. W. *Listening: Its Impact at All Levels on Reading and the Other Language Arts.* Urbana, Ill.: National Council of Teachers of English, 1979.

Mandler, G. "Organization and Memory." In *The Psychology of Learning and Motivation*, edited by K. W. Spence and J. T. Spence. New York: Academic Press, 1967.

Marzano, R. J., R. Brandt, C. Hughes, B. F. Jones, B. Presseissen, S. Rankin, and C. Suhor. *Dimensions of Thinking*. Alexandria, Va.: Association for Supervision and Curriculum Development, in progress.

Mayer, R. E. "Aids to Text Comprehension." *Educational Psychologist* 19 (1984): 30-42.

Mayer, R. E. "Implications of Cognitive Psychology for Instruction in Mathematical Problem Solving." In *Teaching and Learning Mathematical Problem Solving*, edited by E. A. Silver. Hillsdale, N.J.: Erlbaum, 1985.

Meyer, B. J. F. "Reading Research and the Composition Teacher: The Importance of Plans." *College Composition and Communication* 33 (1982): 37-49.

Meyer, B. J. F. "Text Dimensions of Cognitive Processing." In *Learning and Comprehension of Text*, edited by H. Mandl, N. L. Stein, and T. Trabasso. Hillsdale, N.J.: Erlbaum, 1984.

Meyer, B. J. F., D. M. Brandt, and G. S. Bluth. "Use of Top-Level Structure in Text: Key for Reading Comprehension of Ninth-Grade Students." *Reading Research Quarterly* 16 (1980): 72-103.

Michigan State Department of Education, and Michigan State Board of Education. *New Decisions About Reading*. Lansing, Mich.: State Board of Education, 1986.

Nickerson, R. S., D. Perkins, and E. Smith. *Teaching Thinking*. Hillsdale, N.J.: Erlbaum, in press.

O'Keefe, V. P. *Affecting Critical Thinking Through Speech*. Urbana, IL: ERIC Clearinghouse on Reading and Communication Skills; Annandale, Va.: Speech Communication Association, 1986.

Osborn, J., B. F. Jones, and M. Stein. "The Case for Improving Textbooks." *Educational Leadership* 42 (April 1985): 9-17.

Palincsar, A. S., and A. L. Brown. "Reciprocal Teaching of Comprehension-Fostering and Comprehension-Monitoring Activities." *Cognition and Instruction* 1, 2 (1984): 117-175.

Paris, S. G. "Using Classroom Dialogues and Guided Practice to Teach Comprehension Strategies." In *Reading, Thinking, and Conceptual Development*, edited by T. L. Harris and E. J. Cooper. New York: The College Board, 1985.

Paris, S. G., M. Y. Lipson, and K. Wixson. "Becoming a Strategic Reader." *Contemporary Educational Psychology* 8 (1983): 293-316.

Paris, S. G., and P. Winograd. "Metacognition in Academic Learning and Instruction." In *Dimensions of Thinking: Review of Research*, edited by B. F. Jones. Hillsdale, N.J.: Erlbaum, in progress.

Pearson, P. D. *The Comprehension Revolution: A Twenty-Year History of Process and Practice Related to Reading Comprehension* (Reading Education Rep. No. 57). Urbana: University of Illinois, The Center for the Study of Reading, 1985.

Pearson, P. D., and R. J. Tierney. "On Becoming a Thoughtful Reader: Learning to Read Like a Writer." In the *Yearbook of the National Society for the Study of Education, Vol. 83, Part 1, Becoming Readers in a Complex Society*. Chicago: National Society for the Study of Education, 1984.

Pressley, M., J. G. Borkowski, and W. Schneider. "Good Strategy Users Coordinate Metacognition, Strategy Use and Knowledge." In *Annals of Child Development, 4*, edited by R. Vasta and G. Whitehurst, in press.

Polya, G. *How To Solve It*. Princeton, N.J.: Princeton University Press, 1945.

Raphael, T. E., and B. M. Kirscher. *The Effects of Instruction in Compare/Contrast Text Structure on Sixth Grade Students' Reading Comprehension and Writing Products* (Res. Ser. 161). East Lansing: Michigan State University, Institute for Research on Teaching, August 1985.

Resnick, L. B. "Cognitive Science as Educational Research: Why We Need It Now." In National Academy of Education, *Improving Education: Perspectives on Educational Research*. Pittsburgh: University of Pittsburgh, Learning Research and Development Center, 1984.

Resnick, L. B. *Education and Learning to Think*. A special report prepared for the Commission on Behavioral and Social Sciences and Education, National Research Council, 1985.

Roehler, L. M. "Measuring Teachers' Knowledge Structures." Paper presented at the annual meeting of the American Educational Research Association, Washington, D.C., April 1987.

Roth, K. J. "Conceptual Change, Learning, and Student Processing of Science Texts." Paper presented at the annual meeting of the American Educational Research Association, San Francisco, 1985.

Rumelhart, D. E. "Schemata: The Building Blocks of Cognition." In *Theoretical Issues in Reading Comprehension*, edited by R. J. Spiro, B. C. Bruce, and W. F. Brewer. Hillsdale, N.J.: Erlbaum, 1980.

Scardamalia, M., and C. Bereiter. "Research on Written Composition." In *Handbook of Research on Teaching*, 3d ed., edited by M. Wittrock. New York: Macmillan, 1985.

Schoenfeld, A. H. *Mathematical Problem Solving*. New York: Academic Press, 1985.

Schnotz, W. "Comparative Instructional Text Organization." In *Learning and Comprehension of Text*, edited by H. Mandl, N. L. Stein, and T. Trabasso. Hillsdale, N.J.: Erlbaum, 1985.

Segal, J., S. F. Chipman, and R. Glaser, eds. *Thinking and Learning Skills: Relating Instruction to Research, Vol. 1*. Hillsdale, N.J.: Erlbaum, 1985.

Shimmerlik, S. M. "Organization Theory and Memory for Prose: A Review of the Literature." *Review of Educational Research* 48 (1978): 103-121.

Silver, E. A., ed. *Teaching and Learning Mathematical Problem Solving*. Hillsdale, N.J.: Erlbaum, 1985.

Spiro, R. J. "Constructive Processes in Prose Comprehension and Recall." In *Theoretical Issues in Reading Comprehension*, edited by R. J. Spiro, B. C. Bruce, and W. F. Brewer. Hillsdale, N.J.: Erlbaum, 1980.

Stein, N. L., and C. G. Glenn. "An Analysis of Story Comprehension in Elementary School Children." In *New Directions in Discourse Processing*, edited by R. Freedle. Norwood, N.J.: Ablex, 1979.

Sternberg, R. M. "Intelligence, Wisdom, and Creativity: Three is Better Than One." *Educational Psychologist* 21 (1986): 175-190.

Sternberg, R. M. "How Can We Teach Intelligence?" *Educational Leadership* 42 (September 1984): 38-47.

Stubbs, M. *Language and Literacy: The Sociolinguistics of Reading and Writing*. London: Routledge & Kagan Paul, 1980.

Thomas, J. W., and W. D. Rohwer, Jr. "Academic Learning Strategies: The Role of Learning Strategies." *Educational Psychologist* 21 (1986): 19-41.

Thompson, P. W. "Experience, Problem Solving, and Learning Mathematics: Considerations for Developing Mathematics Curricula." In *Teaching and Learning Mathemat-*

ical Problem Solving, edited by E. A. Silver. Hillsdale, N.J.: Erlbaum, 1985.

Tierney, R. J. *Learning from Text* (Reading Education Rep. No. 37). Urbana: University of Illinois, The Center for the Study of Reading, 1983.

Toulmin, S., A. Janik, and R. Rieke. *An Introduction to Reasoning*. New York: Macmillan, 1984.

Van Patten, J. R., C.-I. Chao, and C. M. Reigeluth. "A Review of Strategies for Sequencing and Synthesizing Information." *Review of Educational Research* 56 (1986): 437-472.

Vygotsky, L. S. *Thought and Language*. Cambridge, Mass.: M.I.T. Press, 1962.

Weinstein, C. E., and R. E. Mayer. "The Teaching of Learning Strategies." In *Relating Instruction to Research*, edited by J. Segal, S. Chipman, and R. Glaser. Hillsdale, N.J.: Erlbaum, 1985.

Weinstein, C. E., and V. L. Underwood. "Learning Strategies: The How of Learning." In *Relating Instruction to Research*, edited by J. Segal, S. Chipman, and R. Glaser. Hillsdale, N.J.: Erlbaum, 1985.

Winograd, P. N., and V. C. Hare. "Direct Instruction of Reading Comprehension Strategies: The Nature of Teacher Explanation." In *Learning and Study Strategy Research: Issues in Assessment, Instruction, and Evaluation*, edited by E. Goetz, P. Alexander, and C. Weinstein. New York: Academic Press, in press.

Wisconsin Department of Public Instruction. *A Guide to Curriculum Planning in Reading*, edited by D. Cook. Madison: Wisconsin Department of Public Instruction, 1986.

Wisconsin Instructional Television. *Story Lords*. Madison: Wisconsin Instructional Television, 1985.

Wittrock, M. C. *Generative Reading Comprehension*. Ginn Occasional Reports. Boston: Ginn, 1983.

The Editors

2 Strategic Teaching: A Cognitive Focus

> The decent docent doesn't doze.
> He teaches standing on his toes.
> His students dassn't doze and does,
> And that's what teaching is and was.
> —David McCord
> *What Cheer* (1945)

The little verse above captures the spirit of this chapter. This is a chapter about how teachers teach "on their toes" and induce their students to "do" and not to doze. Being on one's toes has been popularized in the teacher-effects literature as "with-it-ness" and refers to an array of teaching skills, many of which fall under the domains of leadership and management. Considerable evidence suggests that a teacher's ability to allocate the appropriate time for instruction, to provide smooth transitions during the academic day, to generate and consistently apply rules and procedures in the classroom, and to pace instruction enhances the uses of instructional time (Brophy and Good 1986, Duffy 1984). These management activities serve to prepare a sound learning environment and to provide an advantageous position for *strategic teaching*. Thus, the role of management in teaching is an important precursor to strategic teaching.

Strategic teaching extends the notion of with-it-ness to focus on the cognitive activities in which teachers and learners engage. Speaking broadly, strategic teaching is both a role and a process. We will start with the role of the strategic teacher because it is quite different from that of manager. This role derives in part from research on expert teaching (e.g., Berliner 1986, Borko and Niles 1986, Clark and Peterson 1986), in part from research on explicit strategy instruction (e.g., Palincsar and Brown in press), and in part from our observations of what good teachers do.

First, we see the strategic teacher as a *thinker* and *decision maker*. Strategic teachers spend a lot of time thinking about instructional planning and teaching. Figure 2.1 tries to capture both the categories of information that strategic teachers think about as well as the process of planning and teaching. Note that both instructional planning and the act of teaching are thinking processes that involve the same considerations: the better prepared the teacher is, the more smoothly and efficiently the actual process of instruction will proceed.

Second, strategic teachers draw upon a *rich knowledge base*. They really know their subject area, and they have internalized a repertoire of routines, organizational patterns, and teaching/learning strategies that help them to select, sequence, present, and evaluate instructional content. Thus, their wealth of knowledge and experience helps expert teachers deal with the complexity of planning and teaching and enables them to plan and execute sequences of instruction efficiently and effectively.

Third, our vision of the teacher includes a strong emphasis on the teacher as *model* and *mediator*. As model, the teacher frequently demonstrates the process of thinking by thinking aloud and asking students to think aloud about such things as the reasoning in selecting important information or solving a problem. To mediate means to intercede—in this case to intercede between the learner and the learning environment (Feuerstein 1985). As mediator, the strategic teacher helps students to organize and interpret information. Among other things, this means providing adequate support for learning but, at the same time, conceptualizing skills instruction as a *means* of attaining content objectives so that students will ultimately become independent learners.

To summarize, strategic teaching is both a role and a process. It portrays the teacher as constantly thinking and making decisions, as having a rich knowledge base of content and teaching/learning strategies, and as being both a model and mediator in the classroom. In the remainder of this chapter, we discuss various categories of information that form the parameters of strategic teaching: aligning the variables of instruction, relating instruction to learning, developing effective instructional strategies, relating assessment to instruction and learning, and considering key context variables.

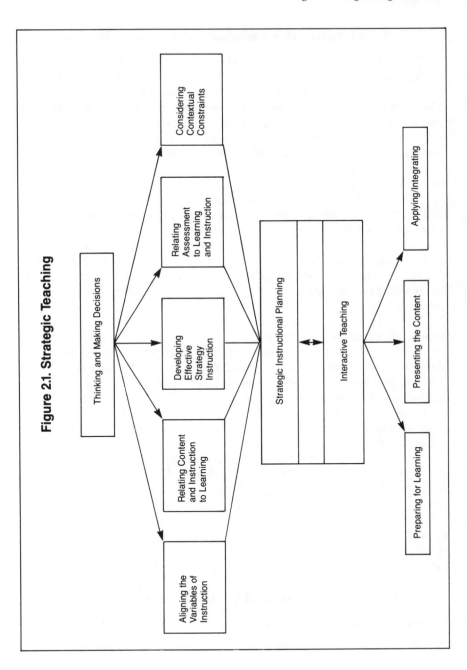

Figure 2.1. Strategic Teaching

Aligning the Variables of Instruction

Our framework suggests that teachers consider at least four variables to develop instruction (Jenkins 1978; Brown, Bransford, Ferrara, and Campione 1983). The first variable, *characteristics of the learner*, includes the students' general fund of knowledge and knowledge about the particular content to be instructed. Also included are the specific strategies available to learners, the flexibility with which they use these strategies, and their attributions about success and failure as learners: that is, the extent to which learners attribute success in school situations to strategic effort as opposed to luck and ability, factors over which we have little control.

The second variable is the *material to be learned*. In most cases, the material is best represented by the textbook used. Characteristics such as careful organization of the material, clarity of presentation, and familiarity of concepts positively influence what students learn. If these features are not present in the instructional materials, both the teacher and the learner face the additional burden of imposing organization on the material, working to clarify the concepts, and building background knowledge to facilitate linking the familiar with the unfamiliar.

The third variable refers to the *criterial task*, or the goals and outcomes the teacher and learner designate. Examples of criterial tasks include skimming for key ideas, writing a play, solving a specific type of problem, memorizing certain formulas, comparing and contrasting key vocabulary terms, and so on.

The final variable, *learning strategies,*refers to the particular goal-directed activities in which the learner engages to achieve the criterial task. The strategic teacher is knowledgeable regarding a repertoire of cognitive strategies and collaborates with his or her students in selecting, applying, and monitoring the use of these strategies to achieve specific learning goals.

These four variables are the "givens" of instruction, the most fundamental elements with which the teacher and curriculum developer must work. They establish the context for instruction, and it is vital that teachers align these variables with each other and with assessment. Strategic teachers work actively to ensure (1) that the teaching/learning strategies, materials, and tests truly address the criterial task; (2) that these variables are consistent in terms of level of difficulty and substance; and (3) most important, that these variables constitute a good "match" with the students' prior knowledge and abilities.

Relating Content and Instruction to Learning

Content Priorities and Considerations of Prior Knowledge

The first consideration of the strategic teacher is to establish what content is to be learned. This is a complex and interactive process that involves evaluating the content in the instructional materials, the quality of the materials, and the students' prior knowledge. Because we have asked four content specialists to apply our model to specific content areas, we will not dwell on issues related to selecting the content or the role of content expertise in strategic teaching.

However, it is important to briefly note that one of the most prominent themes of the literature on expert teaching is the fact that expert teachers are highly knowledgeable about their respective content areas (Clark and Peterson 1986). As with other experts, they are highly cognizant of the organizational patterns and categories of information that are associated with a given content (Berliner 1986). Through a long-term familiarity with teaching particular portions of the content and the process of teaching itself, they have internalized sometimes quite lengthy sequences of instruction that may require only minimal notation for a lesson plan. Strategic teachers also have a fine-grained knowledge of what students know about the content and their available learning strategies, so that they can estimate when they will have to provide more and less support for learning. They have a clear sense of what strategies are most efficient for learning specific segments of content and specific skills (Schoenfeld 1985). All of this knowledge comes into play as strategic teachers establish content priorities.

Organizational Patterns and Learning

Once content priorities are established, the strategic teacher can focus on identifying organizational patterns that will help frame student thinking about the content and will influence considerations about the criterial task. In Chapter 1, we discussed the effects of organizing information on comprehension, recall, and writing. This section describes various strategies for relating the content of the text to student learning. Specifically, we focus on teaching students to use frames and graphic outlines to organize what they read and write.

To recall, frames are sets of questions or categories of information that are fundamental to understanding a given topic (Jones, Tinzmann, Friedman, and Walker 1987). Authors may use frames to organize what they write, but frames are not usually explicit in content texts. Therefore, it may be helpful for the teacher to use these questions, statements, or categories as pattern guides to help students study a text or situation systematically. Frames may be presented before reading or problem solving as an advance organizer, during reading or problem solving to help focus attention on what is important and unimportant, or after a lesson to summarize, sequence, and integrate information.

Graphic outlines are visual maps or representations that reflect key ideas and text structures or organizational patterns that are used in textbooks and student writing. Graphic outlines that may be most recognizable to teachers include semantic webs or spider maps (cf. Heimlich and Pittleman 1986, Herber 1985). These maps have a central node with various levels of branches extending from the node as the legs of a spider extend from its body (hence, the name "spider map"). An example of a spider map is provided in Figure 2.2a. There are, however, many other types of representations in addition to spider maps. Jones (1986) stressed the importance for teachers and students of selecting or constructing graphic outlines that reflect both the content and the pattern suggested by the content. For example, a spider map is most appropriate to describe one thing, such as an object with its attributes and features, a theme with supporting information, a concept with critical features and examples, or a problem with various solutions or consequences. That is, the object, theme, concept, or problem may be placed in the central node with the supporting information on the branches or "legs." However, this structure is less useful when describing a sequence of events or a concept hierarchy. Sequential information, such as the steps in a procedure or a series of events, would better fit into a series of boxes or circles linked by arrows called chains (see Figure 2.2b). Concept hierarchies would best be represented by a structure that clearly depicts the multiple levels of the concepts (see Figure 2.2c).

Graphic organizers and graphic outlining systems with frames and procedures for summarizing can be powerful tools to help students locate, select, sequence, integrate, and restructure information—both from the perspective of understanding and from the perspective of producing information in written responses (e.g., Van Patten, Chao, and Reigeluth 1986). This is evident from the number of graphic outlining systems that have improved comprehension, recall, and writing, referred to in Chapter 1 (e.g., Armbruster, Anderson, and Ostertag 1987).

However, this body of research comes with some cautions and pitfalls. First, while teaching students to use frames, graphics, and summarizing may be highly rewarding, it will take time. Some studies did not show effects without sustained instruction lasting weeks and months. Second, *some* of the systems that are available are very complex or quite specialized for a specific type of information or subject area. It is not clear that either students or teachers would be likely to continue to apply them on a long-term basis without the support of a research study. Third, it is sometimes difficult to apply a given frame, perhaps because it is not the most appropriate structure, or perhaps because imposing organization on unorganized or poorly organized information is just plain hard. Such difficulties are to be expected in processing complex information, especially if the information is from multiple sources.

Analysis of this literature suggests that the most effective studies contained several instructional components:

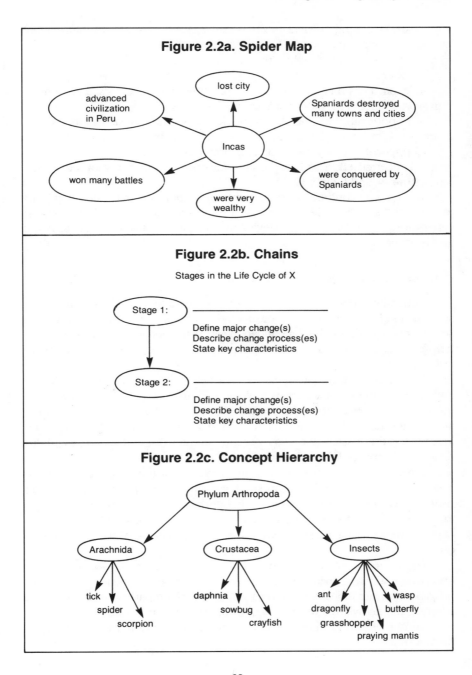

Figure 2.2a. Spider Map

lost city

advanced civilization in Peru

Spaniards destroyed many towns and cities

Incas

won many battles

were conquered by Spaniards

were very wealthy

Figure 2.2b. Chains

Stages in the Life Cycle of X

Stage 1: ———————————

Define major change(s)
Describe change process(es)
State key characteristics

Stage 2: ———————————

Define major change(s)
Describe change process(es)
State key characteristics

Figure 2.2c. Concept Hierarchy

Phylum Arthropoda

Arachnida

Crustacea

Insects

tick
spider
scorpion

daphnia
sowbug
crayfish

ant
dragonfly
grasshopper
wasp
butterfly
praying mantis

1. key structural elements such as the relevant categories of information, questions, or concepts;
2. the appropriate graphic structure(s);
3. where relevant, appropriate rules/procedures for summarization;
4. explicit instruction in how to apply the frames, graphics, and summarizing procedures to a variety of learning situations;
5. opportunities for the class to work as a whole or in small groups with an emphasis on brainstorming and cooperative learning;
6. opportunities for discrimination and transfer; and
7. concerted effort to link the new information to prior knowledge (see Jones, Amiran, and Katims 1985).

When these conditions are present, our experience has been that both teachers and students with whom we have worked generally perceive that the repertoire of organizational strategies they acquire empowers their teaching and learning.

Critical Tasks and the Goals of Learning

Generally speaking, the goals of teaching parallel those of learning. The strategic teacher focuses on the means by which his or her students can construct meaning and can become independent in the enterprise of learning. It is helpful to conceptualize achieving these goals through a series of criterial tasks.

After selecting the content, the strategic teacher's first concern is to identify and prioritize the specific purposes of learning. In strategy instruction there is, in fact, a dual agenda to which the teacher attends. The purposes of learning are defined not only by the content or domain-specific knowledge that the learner should possess but also by the techniques or strategies that will enhance the learning of this content.

Turning first to the content, multiple levels of learning need to be considered (Brown and Palincsar in press). For example, one purpose of learning may be the *retention of facts*. This is a rather restricted definition of learning in that what is learned might enable one to pass a test but does not become a part of the learner's usable bank of knowledge to be adapted, applied, and modified over time.

The retention of facts can be contrasted with the *assimilation of new knowledge*. When knowledge is assimilated, it is owned by the learner and can be applied to situations that are relatively novel in comparison to the situation in which the knowledge was first acquired. Assimilation involves making inferences and integrating information for understanding rather than simply remembering.

Another level of learning, modification or adaptation of assimilated knowledge, occurs when the learner is confronted by a new experience that forces this alteration or refinement. This level of learning is referred to as *restructuring* or *conceptual change*. Each succeeding level of learning is more empowering to the student because with each level the learner is allocated more responsibility and achieves more independence from the teacher.

To return to the main theme of this section, the strategic teacher recognizes the various levels at which selected content can be learned and that the level achieved by students is no accident. As a teacher plans for the actual instruction, student strategies become critical. Content learning will depend on how students can learn.

Strategy Instruction

This brings us to the teacher's second agenda. What strategies are needed to learn the content? How will the students know how to use them? What instruction is needed?

Strategies represent a diverse array of activities that researchers continue to identify and validate. Weinstein and Mayer (1986), for example, have suggested a taxonomy of strategies including: (1) affective strategies that serve to focus attention, minimize anxiety, and maintain motivation; (2) strategies that serve to monitor learning such as self-questioning and error detection; and (3) strategies that serve to organize information, such as clustering and outlining, including graphic outlining. The goal of strategy instruction is to foster independence on the part of the learner.

To achieve this goal, it is important that students acquire several dimensions of information about the strategies they use. Clearly, students need to know what the strategy is (*declarative information*), how to apply it (*procedural knowledge*), as well as when and where to use the strategy (*conditional knowledge*). Yet, frequently, school objectives and tests ask for students to demonstrate their knowledge of a skill by actively using it in a school task, without asking them to demonstrate that they know what the skill or strategy is, or that they know when to use it or why it works. Moreover, in traditional instruction, students may have little opportunity to demonstrate that they can discriminate when one strategy is more appropriate than another or that they can modify their behavior when learning conditions change or when learning problems arise. Strategic teachers try to provide such opportunities for students.

The decision as to what strategies to teach, however, cannot be made in isolation from the decision regarding what the content is and what level of learning is desired. To illustrate, if the goal of instruction is the retention of French vocabulary words, a mnemonic strategy that assists rote learning (e.g., the keyword method—Pressley and Levin 1983) would be an appropriate strategy to impart to the students, and the learning outcome would be appropriately assessed with a matching task. If the goal of instruction is integration and assimilation, the mnemonic strategy might still be appropriate, but the outcome would be assessed in another way, such as student-generated conversation or writing. Finally, if the goal were restructuring of knowledge or conceptual change, the mnemonic strategy would no longer be sufficient. Restructuring, which could be assessed by having students identify the meanings of words with which they have had no prior experience, would be better achieved by teaching students to recognize the derivation of words and word families and to use context clues. Figure 2.3 illustrates this dual agenda between content and strategy outcomes.

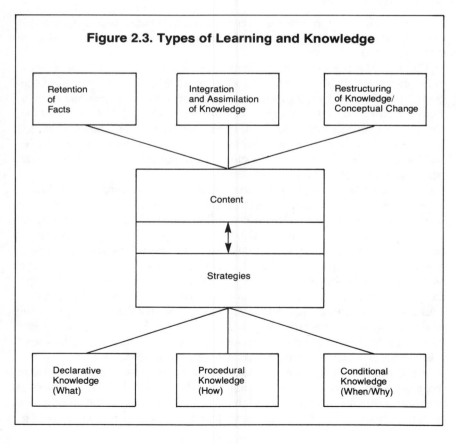

Figure 2.3. Types of Learning and Knowledge

| Retention of Facts | Integration and Assimilation of Knowledge | Restructuring of Knowledge/ Conceptual Change |

Content

Strategies

| Declarative Knowledge (What) | Procedural Knowledge (How) | Conditional Knowledge (When/Why) |

To summarize, the goals of a given sequence of instruction are defined by the content to be learned and by the level of learning to be achieved. While the content may be determined by the curriculums or texts adopted by a school district, it is the learning strategies in which the students engage that will determine the level of learning achieved. This dual agenda suggests that the strategic teacher attends not only to the product of learning but to the process in which the learner is engaged as well. It is attention to the process of learning that will foster self-regulation on the part of the learner. The cognitive and metacognitive strategies that the learner uses in this process and the ways in which these strategies are addressed in instruction are discussed in the next section.

Cognitive and Metacognitive Strategies

What, according to research, can help teachers and schools make decisions about strategy instruction? As noted in Chapter 1, many themes emerge from the literature on teaching and learning specific skills. While all the themes are supported by research, not all of them are consistent. Moreover, we have to say "up front" that making decisions about who receives skills instruction, what skills are selected, and how they are sequenced into the curriculum has as much to do with personal values about equity and philosophy of pedagogy as it does with knowledge of research. The few remarks that follow, therefore, reflect our ideological commitments as well as our knowledge of research and are not intended as conclusive or emerging strictly from research.

Should all students receive explicit strategy instruction? If students do not have an appropriate strategy for learning a specific content objective, then teaching such a strategy is likely to enhance achievement, especially for less proficient students and younger students. Furthermore, since low-achieving students are not likely to develop effective cognitive and metacognitive strategies spontaneously, it is important to provide learning situations enhanced by explicit strategy instruction, particularly for tasks requiring restructuring, complex reasoning, and sustained mental activity. On the other hand, if the students already have an efficient strategy for learning a skill or a given type of content, explicit strategy instruction may actually hinder achievement—perhaps an occasion to consider the adage, "If it isn't broken, don't fix it." In a later section of this chapter we discuss how to determine if students have acquired a given strategy or skill.

What skills should be selected for instruction? Here the answer is even fuzzier, and we recognize that there are as many answers to this question as there are teachers, researchers, and administrators. Speaking broadly, an implication of research throughout this chapter is that selection of skills should be based on appropriateness to specific tasks needed for success in school and in life.

43

Thus, we support the principle that the selection of strategies and skills should be "content driven." Accordingly, our preference, both in content courses and in study skill courses, is always to relate specific strategies and skills to cognitive tasks such as comprehending a passage, composing an essay, making a decision, solving a problem, creating a play, and so on. This principle contrasts sharply with the widespread practice of teaching skills as ends in themselves.

With regard to choosing specific skills for inclusion in a given sequence of instruction, we would refer the reader to Planning Guide 1 in Chapter 1. This list represents our "best shot" at selecting skills that currently have a sound research base.

How should skills be sequenced? Here there is greater consensus for teaching skills holistically, rather than breaking a given skill down into a series of subskills. Yet there are no hard and fast rules for defining the ideal level of generality that distinguishes a skill from a subskill. Again, we would refer the reader to Planning Guide 1 for examples. We would also refer the reader to the description of instructional strategies for the various phases of learning and teaching.

The Phases of Strategic Teaching

Throughout this volume, we will make reference to three phases of instruction: *preparation for learning, presentation of content to be learned,* and *application and integration of new knowledge.* These phases parallel the phases of learning that we discussed in Chapter 1 and are defined by the instructional objective(s). For example, in preparation for learning a new type of mathematics problem, the teacher may want the students to recall the algorithm used in solving an analogous type of problem to which they have already been exposed. This might be followed by demonstrating the algorithm to be employed in the new problem type (the presentation). Finally, the teacher might present the students with a series of problems, some requiring use of the novel algorithm and others to be solved by applying established algorithms. This task requires that the student discriminate among problem types and correctly apply the appropriate algorithm.

It is not our plan to be prescriptive with regard to the appropriate strategies for each phase of instruction. In fact, it would be folly to suggest that we have the knowledge to be prescriptive. Rather, the strategic teacher acquires a repertoire of strategies to share with students and selects the appropriate strategy(ies) according to the goals that have been defined for instruction and then evaluates the merits of the strategy according to the success the students have achieved. In the following section, we will illustrate how a repertoire of strategies might be implemented in the three phases of instruction.

Preparation for learning. Ms. Jackson's first graders have been told that they are going to hear a story about a little boy who wanted a dog very badly but whose parents would not permit him to get one. The children have been paired off and are telling one another about things that they have wanted but could not have and what they did in an attempt to get what they wanted. Mr. Phillips' class of fifth graders is beginning a unit on the Sahara Desert. His students are completing a semantic map of the word "desert" on the board. They have indicated the characteristics of the desert, named deserts with which they are familiar, and identified concepts, such as irrigation, that they associate with the desert. The students in tenth-grade literature are about to read and critique a mystery of their choosing. Before they begin reading, Ms. Pfeiffer has asked the students to recall mystery stories they have read or seen enacted that they particularly enjoyed. She is eliciting from the students the elements and organization of a successful mystery.

In each of these examples, the class is engaged in an activity that will activate prior knowledge and provide the opportunity to achieve an interface between the schemata or knowledge structures already available to the learner and the new information that will be presented. In addition, this type of activity permits the teacher to assess the quality of the background knowledge learners possess. Such an evaluation helps the teacher determine how much support students will require in learning the new material. Furthermore, research conducted by Anderson and his colleagues (Anderson this volume; Anderson, Smith, and Ross 1985) and Alvermann, Smith, and Readence (1985) informs us that students who are naive or who possess partial or incorrect knowledge about concepts tend to recast new information they encounter to conform to their prior knowledge, unless there is some intervention by the teacher that helps the students to reconcile new and old information.

The above examples illustrate clearly the many ways teachers can prepare students for the presentation of new content. To assist teachers in selecting specific strategies to prepare for learning, we would like to describe a procedure investigated by Langer (1984) with students in grades three through graduate school. While Langer refers to the procedures as PReP (PreREading Plan), the reader will readily see that the procedure would be useful in the presentation of new concepts regardless of the medium (e.g., text, lecture, film). The purpose of PReP is to draw upon the knowledge that students already possess about a topic and have them reflect on the appropriateness of these ideas. The teacher prepares for PReP by selecting concepts that are central to the understanding of the new information to be learned and that can be represented by words, phrases, or pictures. The teacher then engages the students in three activities:

1. Elicits initial association with the concept—"Tell me anything that

comes to mind when you think of. . . ." The teacher accepts all responses in a nonjudgmental manner and records them on the board or on an overhead.

2. Generates reflection on initial associations—"What made you think of . . . ?" This helps the students become aware of what they know and judge whether it is likely that this information is relevant to what they will be learning. Listening and interacting with other members of the group helps the students build upon what they already know.

3. Leads the students in refining and reformulating their knowledge: "Based on our discussion, have you any new ideas about . . . ?"

At the conclusion of the three activities, the students are oriented to the new content to be learned, and the teacher and students are aware of the knowledge or conceptions possessed regarding the content at hand. The application of this instructional activity in social studies is clearly presented in the chapter by Alvermann (this volume).

Langer (1984) also provides suggestions regarding how teachers can evaluate the quality of students' background knowledge while assessing its quantity. She suggests that student knowledge can be categorized into three levels of organization. First, if students are able to provide definitions or analogies for concepts presented, or are able to link various concepts, this suggests that their knowledge is fairly *well organized*. The instructional implication is that the students will require minimal guidance as the new information is presented. Second, when the students provide examples, describe attributes, or define certain aspects of the concepts, their knowledge is *somewhat organized* and additional instructional assistance is indicated. Finally, if the students are able to make only tangential or superficial remarks, or if they recall first-hand experiences that may be only remotely relevant to the topic, then their knowledge is *diffusely organized*, suggesting the need for considerable instructional support. This assessment helps the strategic teacher adjust instruction to build from the students' present knowledge.

Planning Guide 3 at the end of this chapter suggests a variety of activities that teachers and students can use to prepare for new learning. The reader will note that many of the same activities can be directed by either the teacher or a student. For example, a teacher can provide a structured guide, similar to an outline, that highlights the important content to be presented (e.g., in a lecture), or the students can generate such an outline. For example, when using the SPaRCS procedure (Survey/Predict, Read/Construct, Summarize) (Jones 1986), the students are, at first, guided to survey the features of the text using titles and subtitles, as well as the graphics and any other organizers that the text might provide. This skimming activity serves as a stimulus to make inferences about the text structure and topic. Using the information obtained in these two steps, students generate specific questions or categories that are used to predict the content and establish a purpose for reading. Having generated their own advance organizers (with teacher guidance), the students are prepared to relate personal experiences or prior learning to the anticipated learning by engaging in the same type of brainstorming suggested in PReP. The goal here, over a period of time, is to have the students internalize the questions and categories associated with specific text structures and topics and learn to use this information in independent preparatory activities (e.g., Armbruster et al. 1987).

The extent to which the preparatory activity is teacher- or student-led depends on a number of factors, including, of course, whether the information will be presented via text or lecture. In addition, students' prior experiences and knowledge regarding the content will influence the extent to which they can prepare for learning independently of the teacher. In the spirit of inducing students to be autonomous learners and thinkers, it is to the students' advantage that they be taught and encouraged to activate background knowledge independently, anticipate new content, inquire as to the best means of organizing the material to be presented, and define specific purposes for new learning. It is evident, however, that low-achieving students are likely to require greater support and practice in their efforts to become independent.

Further examples of strategies used to activate and link prior knowledge may be found in each of the content area chapters in Part II. In Alvermann's chapter, the focus is on teaching vocabulary to build knowledge that may be missing but is prerequisite to constructing meaning for the new social studies content. In Anderson's and Linquist's chapters, the focus is on eliciting conceptions and beliefs to ascertain and perhaps change specific knowledge structures that already exist but may be in error. Beach emphasizes how prior experiences serve as a lens through which to interpret literature.

Presentation of content to be learned. In many respects, the activity that occurs during the presentation phase of instruction represents a continuation of what was initiated during the preparation phase. The objectives at this time include confirming and refining predictions, clarifying ideas, and, of course, constructing meaning for the newly presented information.

Historically, analyzers of instruction have emphasized teacher activity and neglected the role of the student. The teacher pours out information and the student passively receives it. There is no question but that the source of the information, whether it be a text, movie, or computer program, can serve to enhance or impede the acquisition of new knowledge; yet it is in fact the student who makes this information meaningful. It is the student who must select the relevant ideas, compare the new ideas with previously held concepts, organize and integrate this new knowledge, and monitor for understanding of the new information, taking appropriate remedial measures when there has been a breakdown in comprehension.

It is only within the last decade that cognitive instructional research has systematically investigated how student-teacher interaction can promote this type of processing *during* the learning of new information. Illustrative is the work of Palincsar and Brown (1984; in press), who have investigated the use of an instructional technique called reciprocal teaching. Reciprocal teaching is a dialogue among students and teachers for the purpose of jointly constructing the meaning of text. The dialogue is structured with the use of four strategies that students are encouraged to engage in recursively while reading. The strategies include: question generating, summarizing, monitoring for and clarifying concepts or vocabulary that might be unclear, and predicting upcoming content based on the clues provided in the text (e.g., through the organization of the text, author's use of embedded questions, or subheadings).

In reciprocal teaching, teachers and students take turns assuming the role of teacher and leading the discussion. The dialogue permits the adult teacher the opportunity to model how he or she uses these strategies to process the text and to decide and remember what is useful in the text. This dialogue also permits the students to demonstrate how well they are able to employ the strategies while the teacher coaches them in their processing of the text. The eventual goal is, of course, to enable the students to internalize the use of these strategies and be able to construct meaning independently.

The instructional heuristic during the presentation phase suggests that the teacher identify the cognitive demands of the task, consider effective cognitive processes to meet these demands, and model with the students the use of these cognitive processes.

Application and Integration. The instructional activities in which we engage during this phase are again related to the criterial task. The driving question during this phase becomes, "Has the goal of learning been met, and if not, what further activity is appropriate?" It is for this reason that the instructional activities during this phase are often evaluative. For example, students are asked to respond to a series of questions, to solve a problem using information presented regarding an analogous situation, or to summarize and critique the newly presented information. While these techniques are indeed evaluative in nature, they also provide the opportunity for students to integrate and extend their learning. It is at this point that students should achieve closure; the various pieces are integrated to form the larger picture.

During this phase of instruction, the students are induced to compare and contrast the new information or skill that has been acquired with former knowledge or procedures. Such activity suggests that this phase is also one of *conceptual change* (Anderson this volume) or *restructuring* (Bereiter and Scardamalia 1984). Prior concepts are refined or perhaps abandoned in favor of new concepts, depending upon the degree of congruence between the new and the old. The process of referring back to information discussed during the preparation for learning phase suggests that strategic teaching is nonlinear, which reflects the nonlinear nature of most thinking and problem-solving activity.

This process is well accounted for in the teaching technique called K-W-L (Ogle 1986). K-W-L involves the completion of a work sheet to reflect: (1) what the students *Know* about a concept; (2) what they *Want* to learn about the concept; and (3) what they have *Learned* about the concept. The K and W activities occur prior to the presentation of new information and can be accomplished through teacher-led discussion. The final step, however, is student-initiated as the students document what they have learned, answering many of the questions indicated under "what I want to learn," and generate new questions stimulated by the new material. Assessing what has been learned may also initiate conceptual change as students compare what they have learned with previous learnings. Additionally, in K-W-L Plus, developed more recently, the students may use frame and graphic organizers to summarize what they have learned.

Another example of a teacher-led activity useful in this phase of learning and instruction is the completion of a pattern guide (Jones 1986). The skeleton of the pattern guide can be constructed to reflect identification of cause and effect, problem and solution, comparisons and contrasts, or temporal sequencing, depending on the nature of the material and criterial task.

Initially, the teacher identifies the organizational pattern and is responsible for guiding students to frame questions and graphic outlines to integrate various parts of the text or problem. This process is typically highly interactive, with much questioning and brainstorming to determine the key categories and questions. In fact, consistent evidence indicates that constructing graphic organizers and outlines is more effective when done as a social activity involving the whole class or small groups, rather than when it is completed as an individual assignment (e.g., Darch, Carnine, and Kameenui 1986).

Determining the best graphic structure to represent information is sometimes a matter of trial and error and sometimes a matter of choice. That is, in conceptualizing information with many elements such as the story of the Pilgrims, the teacher may select among various text structures and frames such as the sequence of events when the Pilgrims fled Europe and landed in America, the various problems and solutions they encountered, or a comparison of Pilgrim and native American traditions. Once the information is in a graphic representation, however, it may be used to structure an oral or written summary. Jones, Amiran, and Katims (1985), for example, developed a framework for analyzing and summarizing information in matrices. Specifically, the row and column headings may be used in an introductory paragraph. Row generalizations are then used as topic sentences in essays, and column generalizations are used to stimulate conclusions and summary remarks. These principles apply to other types of structures as well. Figures 2.4 and 2.5 provide examples of graphics that were used to generate summaries. Note how the questions generated for the interaction frame graphics are used to structure the summary.

After completing the basic learning, teachers may want to apply the newly acquired knowledge to new learning situations to consolidate learning. Solving new problems and creating dramatic or visual artifacts, for example, relate the content to other activities. In the description above about the Pilgrims, the older students might compare the study of the Pilgrims or the study of the Jews in Europe to Palestineans today.

Recursive and Nonlinear Teaching

An important feature of all the strategies we have described is that they have elements that are recursive and nonlinear. That is, throughout the phases of learning, strategic teaching provides opportunities for the learner to pause and reflect, to think back to previous ideas, and to compare new and old information as well as to anticipate what is to come.

*   *   *

To summarize, strategic teachers have a dual agenda as they consider how to relate content and instruction to learning. They must balance a focus on content priorities with strategy instruction not only as they plan sequences of instruction but also during the act of teaching in the classroom. When strategic teachers identify content goals, they also consider the strategies that students need to use to learn the content well. These strategies then become secondary instructional goals to be incorporated as an integral part of the criterial task(s).

Some of these strategies involve using organizational patterns and graphic representations of text. Others involve cognitive skills such as predicting, questioning, and summarizing. Still other strategies are metacognitive, involving self-regulation of learning. A critical aspect of strategic planning and instruction is to organize instruction so that both content and strategy objectives are addressed in each phase of learning. It is also important to provide opportunities for students to "think back" in order to link what they are learning to prior knowledge or to test early predictions as well as to anticipate what is to come. We described a number of generic instructional strategies that integrate these features of instruction: PReP, K-W-L, and SPaRCS. (Additionally, readers are referred to some of the excellent new textbooks oriented to practitioners, such as Singer and Donlan 1985.)

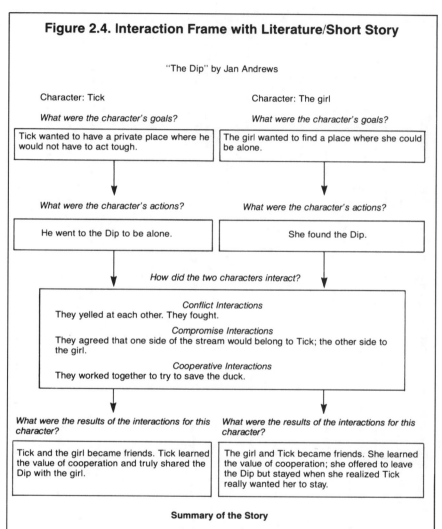

Figure 2.4. Interaction Frame with Literature/Short Story

"The Dip" by Jan Andrews

Character: Tick

What were the character's goals?

Tick wanted to have a private place where he would not have to act tough.

Character: The girl

What were the character's goals?

The girl wanted to find a place where she could be alone.

What were the character's actions?

He went to the Dip to be alone.

What were the character's actions?

She found the Dip.

How did the two characters interact?

Conflict Interactions
They yelled at each other. They fought.

Compromise Interactions
They agreed that one side of the stream would belong to Tick; the other side to the girl.

Cooperative Interactions
They worked together to try to save the duck.

What were the results of the interactions for this character?

Tick and the girl became friends. Tick learned the value of cooperation and truly shared the Dip with the girl.

What were the results of the interactions for this character?

The girl and Tick became friends. She learned the value of cooperation; she offered to leave the Dip but stayed when she realized Tick really wanted her to stay.

Summary of the Story

The Dip was a place in the woods that Tick Merrick had found where he could be alone and be himself and not act tough. One day a girl showed up who also wanted to be alone in the Dip. For a while Tick and the girl fought with each other over the Dip. Neither wanted to leave, so finally they agreed that each could stay but on separate sides of the stream. Their dislike for each other was forgotten when they found an injured duck and tried to nurse it back to health together. The duck did not survive, but Tick and the girl had learned the value of cooperation and found they had become real friends.

Reprinted with permission of the National Education Association.

51

Figure 2.5. Model Matrix and Summary for "Insect-Eating Plants"

INSECT-EATING PLANTS: MATRIX

	VENUS FLY TRAP	PITCHER PLANT	SUNDEW
LOCATION	Coastal marshes, N. and S. America	Various parts of U.S.—bogs/ marshes	No description
GENERAL APPEARANCE	Small, 12 leaves in circle on ground, stem with blossoms	Author does not describe	Very small, size of button/pincushion
CATCH/LURE MECHANISM	Outer ends of leaves hinged w/spines on edges; secretes sweet liquid	Horn-shaped leaves; glands secrete sweet material	Red leaves like spoons; covered with hairs like flypaper
CATCH/LURE PROCESS	1. Insect presses trigger hairs, 2. Red center of leaf secretes liquid, 3. Hinge closes/ traps bug, 4. Digestive juice dissolves bug.	Insects go for material, Get caught in neck hairs, Struggle/slip, Drug makes bug unconscious.	Bugs stick on hairs, Struggle/get stuck, Hairs bend to pin bug, Digested—how?

Notes:

1. The matrix format makes it visually clear how many things are being compared and how many categories of information are discussed by the author.

2. It is also evident at a glance what information is missing; e.g., the author does not really describe the general appearance of the pitcher plant, nor is it clear how the sundew plant digests the insects.

3. Parallel information to be analyzed is physically adjacent in the various cells and rows, facilitating analysis. In this particular matrix, it is likely that the reader might have drawn different conclusions about the similarities and differences among the plants had the information been diagrammed in a semantic map because the relevant information would not have been parallel and easy to read.

INSECT-EATING PLANTS: MODEL SUMMARY

The author describes three insect-eating plants found in marshes and bogs in various parts of the U.S.: the Venus fly trap, the pitcher plant, and the sundew. The article focuses on three categories of information: what the plant looks like, what features of the plant trap insects, and the process of catching and digesting insects. Throughout this passage, the author states that each of the three plants is quite different in the way that it catches and eats insects. However, it seems that the plants catch and eat insects in much the same way, although they look quite different.

In terms of general appearance, each of the three insect-eating plants is strikingly different. The Venus fly trap has small leaves that lie in a circle on the ground, whereas the pitcher plant has leaves shaped like horns with a canopy over the opening. The sundew is tiny, only as large as a button, with reddish leaves that look like spoons around the stem.

In spite of these differences, all three plants have hairlike features and special fluids for trapping and eating insects. The Venus fly trap has hairlike spines around the edges of the leaves and fluids that digest the insects. The pitcher plant has hairs inside the hornlike leaves that secrete a sweet material to catch the insects, a drug that makes the insects unconscious, and digestive juices to digest the insects. The sundew plant has hairs around the edges of the spoon-shaped leaves, and each leaf has a drop of liquid that acts like flypaper. Additionally, there appear to be some digestive fluids.

The process of catching and eating the insects is also quite similar for each of the plants. All three plants trap the insect first, using the hairs and sticky fluids. Then, once the insect is trapped, its struggle to get free traps it further in all three plants. Also, as the trapped insect struggles, digestive juices begin to digest it. The only major difference among the plants in how they catch and eat insects seems to be that the Venus fly trap and the sundew plants move their parts to help trap the insect, whereas the pitcher plant does not move; instead, it traps insects by its shape (the long, slippery canopy and false windows) and the drug it secretes to make the insect unconscious.

In conclusion, the plants do have important differences that distinguish them from each other and from noninsect-eating plants. However, the plants seem to have similar mechanisms and processes for catching and eating insects.

From *Teaching Reading as Thinking* (Facilitator's Manual), Alexandria, Va.: ASCD and NCREL, 1986.

Developing Effective Strategy Instruction

Just as we have suggested that one cannot be prescriptive with regard to what strategies are appropriate during the phases of learning, the same is true of the instructional processes the teacher uses. There are, however, general guidelines suggested by instructional research, which we will discuss at this point.

Assessing Strategy Use

Generally, a good first step is to determine if the students are currently using a strategy in the learning situation and what that strategy is. We know that efficient learners do, in fact, use strategies (c.f. Bereiter and Bird 1985), while less successful learners may choose an inefficient strategy or may be unaware of the need to use a strategy. For example, poor readers often report that the way to prepare for a test is to "read and reread" (Brown and Lawton in progress). The mere repetition of reading is unlikely to produce increments in comprehension and retention if what is read is not understood.

How does one get students to divulge the activity they engage in while learning? One successful means is to have the students think aloud the process they are using. For example, Bird (Bereiter and Bird 1985) had students think aloud as they processed pieces of text, while Scardamalia and Bereiter (1984) had students think aloud while they planned a composition. Sometimes students, particularly older students, are reluctant to engage in "think alouds." In this case a more successful approach might be to interview the students, asking them what advice they would give to a younger student engaged in a similar activity. For a more systematic assessment, Weinstein and her colleagues have developed a test to assess the use of specific learning strategies (see Weinstein and Underwood 1985).

Explaining the Strategy

After evaluating the learning strategy the students are currently using, the teacher is ready to present the proposed strategy. The work of Duffy and Roehler and their colleagues (1986) suggests that what teachers do at this time has tremendous bearing on what students learn. In their experimental work, these authors found that when teachers explicitly informed their students about: (1) what strategy they were learning (declarative information), (2) how they should employ the strategy (procedural information), and (3) in what context they should employ the strategy (conditional information), the students indicated greater awareness of what they were learning and why. In addition, these students performed better on achievement measures than did students whose

53

teachers did not fully inform them regarding these aspects of strategy use.

Having provided this information regarding the targeted strategy(ies), the teacher is ready to provide instruction about strategy use (i.e., procedural knowledge). Interestingly, this is a step at which teachers are frequently not as helpful as they might be. For example, it is not uncommon to urge students to summarize, outline the most important ideas, and underline the topic sentences, but to provide no information regarding how one goes about determining what is important, what constitutes a topic sentence, and so forth.

To guard against this possibility, it is helpful for the teacher to reflect on the processes and skills necessary to implement the strategy(ies) successfully and to provide relevant instruction. For example, in the process of teaching summarization as a strategy, teachers can call students' attention to such procedures as those investigated by Day and Brown (1981):

1. determine if there is a topic sentence that represents the gist of the material,
2. invent a topic sentence if one is not present,
3. name lists or steps (identify a superordinate),
4. delete what is trivial, and
5. delete what is redundant.

After these steps or processes have been taught, they can be integrated, demonstrated, and practiced as a strategy and in the appropriate context.

Modeling the Strategy

Typically, the teacher demonstrates or models the use of the strategy. For example, a mathematics teacher may choose to demonstrate the solution of a division problem by placing the problem on the board and thinking aloud while working through its solution, making remarks such as: "What type of problem is this? This sign indicates to me that this is a division problem. Now that I recognize this is a division problem, what is the first step I should take?" Once again, the focus is on modeling the thinking processes.

Scaffolding the Instruction

While the explanation, instruction, and modeling that have been described thus far are critical to the success of cognitive strategy instruction, they actually represent only the initial steps in such instruction. If students are expected to be able to apply these strategies independently, they must be given the opportunity to practice and demonstrate their use of the strategies.

The role of the teacher in this phase of instruction has been compared to that of a scaffold. Scaffolding has been described as a "process that enables a child or novice to solve a problem, carry out a task, or achieve a goal which would be beyond his unassisted efforts" (Wood, Bruner, and Ross 1976, p. 90). The teacher scaffolds during strategy instruction by *supporting* the students' attempts to use the strategy, providing additional instruction and modeling as the need indicates. The support the teacher provides is *adjusted* according to the learning characteristics, nature of the material, and nature of the criterial tasks. For example, some students may require little more than prompting in the use of the strategy, whereas other students might require further modeling. Regardless of how the support is adjusted, it is regarded as *temporary*. The teacher proceeds to remove the support as the student shows increased competence.

There are several ways support is provided. One is by structuring the task so that the demands increase gradually. Another is to keep the level of difficulty constant and begin with a substantial amount of support, which is later faded. (For a discussion of this issue, see Collins, Brown, and Newman in press.) Still another means of support is to help students articulate the conditions under which the strategy is most useful (Bransford, Sherwood, Vye, and Rieser 1986; Schoenfeld 1985). While we generally think of support provided verbally, students can also be provided with visual prompts to aid them through the task: for example, cards picturing or listing the steps of a strategy (Bereiter and Scardamalia 1984), or a graphic representation of text (Holley and Dansereau 1984). Regardless of the nature of the support, the aim is to remove the support gradually. This gradual ceding of responsibility for employing the strategy promotes the likelihood that the student will internalize and independently apply the strategy. Whether students actually internalize this responsibility, however, depends on their attitudes and beliefs as much as it does on the instructional strategy. Thus, motivation is a central concern of strategic teachers.

Relating Cognitive Strategy Instruction to Motivation

In our discussion of self-regulated learning, we have placed an emphasis on helping students identify and manage the cognitive processes essential to success with learning. However, another dimension of self-regulation cannot be overlooked: the role of motivation. Paris and Oka (1986) described this as the "skill and will" to learn, which increasingly is being considered a part of metacognition in the research literature (e.g., Paris and Winograd in progress). Teachers are well aware of the significance of this issue, and student disinterest plays a prominent role in teachers' discussion of why students fail to learn.

To understand the role of will better, it is helpful to consider cognitive theories of motivation in which attributions and perceptions of self-competence play a significant role. These theories suggest that students' expectations regarding success and failure, in hand with the extent to which they value the learning task, determine the amount of effort they are willing to expend as well as the degree to which they will persist in a learning activity.

Students' expectations regarding success and failure are derived from their previous experiences with learning tasks. Children who have experienced repeated failure often develop an attitude of helplessness and passivity with regard to learning (Seligman 1975, Torgesen 1982). They attribute failure to their lack of ability and do not acknowledge the role of effort in academic success.

One of the principal goals of strategy training is to alter students' beliefs about themselves by teaching them that their failures can be attributed to the lack of effective strategies rather than to the lack of ability or to laziness. By providing students not merely with a backlog of success experiences but with experiences in which they see the effects of strategic effort, it is possible to change students' expectations for success and failure and to help them sustain strategy use (Borkowski, Johnston, and Reid 1986).

Relating Assessment to Learning and Instruction

Measuring the Effectiveness of Learning and Instruction

Traditional means of assessment have typically sought to measure the acquisition of specific information without inquiring as to the cognitive means by which students arrive at these understandings. This is not to suggest that teachers should focus on assessment of strategies such as developing a battery of strategy tests (though we are not opposed to using such tests for diagnostic purposes; see Weinstein and Underwood 1985). To the contrary, just as strategic teachers have a dual agenda with regard to instruction, so, too, they have a dual agenda with regard to assessment. While it is not within the scope of this book to consider assessment extensively, it is important to consider some key issues. First is the need to develop items that assess the various levels of learning. Historically, testing throughout this country has focused on assessing the retention of isolated facts and skills that may not facilitate cognitive development or conceptual change. Second, it is vital to align the level of assessment with the level of learning. That is, if the criterial task involves assimilation of knowledge, then the assessment should demonstrate that students have in fact integrated the new learning. Third, there is the serious problem of the lack of available models, though it is encouraging to see the development of new tests in the area of reading such as those being developed in Michigan and Illinois (see Chapter 1) as well as new tests for measuring thinking skills in the classroom (e.g., Arter and Salmon 1986; Stiggins, Rubel, and Quellmaz 1986).

56

Turning back to the issue of assessing strategies, one means of measuring the acquisition of cognitive strategies involves requesting students to think aloud while completing the task of interest or, for those students who are reluctant to think aloud, asking them to tutor a peer on the completion of the task.

Another means of conducting this assessment is to determine the students' ability to apply the instructed strategy in a learning situation similar to the one in which the strategy has been learned. In research currently in progress, second-grade teachers are conducting reciprocal teaching as a listening comprehension activity, and Palincsar and Brown (1986) are trying to determine the extent to which the students spontaneously use the same comprehension monitoring strategies in their reading activity. The data to date suggest that while some students do appear to apply the strategies spontaneously across the two activities, other students require prompting to do so, and others require instruction regarding how to do this.

Assessment has four important functions in cognitive instruction. First, it provides opportunities for students to consolidate learning and for teachers to ask questions that challenge the learner to integrate the various components of what has been learned and to apply that knowledge. Second, it informs the direction of future learning, not only to remediate what still needs to be learned but also to raise further questions about the extent of learning. Third, it determines the extent to which the instruction is successful and indicates the need to modify the instruction if, in fact, it does not appear to be effective (i.e., it suggests the need to increase the support of the scaffold). Fourth, it demonstrates to students the payoffs for using the strategies.

Besides assessing their students, teachers may also wish to assess the effectiveness of long-range instructional goals by asking themselves the following questions: (1) Are my students in control of their own learning as a result of my instruction? (2) Can students use the knowledge and strategies with increasingly difficult material? (3) Can students transfer their learning to new situations?

Establishing Standards of Excellence

In addition to assessing cognitive processes used in learning, teachers must also direct attention toward establishing criteria for standards of excellence students must meet in completing tasks. The purpose of this endeavor is to ascertain what level of competence is required before a task can be considered to have been completed successfully. Levels of accountability involve several variables: student ability, importance of the task, the frequency of the review, and the focus of the lesson. After the teacher considers the importance of each variable, a balanced measure of accountability has been attained.

Considering Contextual Factors

While it is not within the scope of this chapter to focus on context issues, it is important to consider briefly two major factors that may shape classroom instruction and learning opportunities in significant ways. First, curriculum and testing "drive" instruction in numerous ways but especially in the selection of content and skills that are taught. This may be a problem in schools in which the curriculum or tests focus on mastery of numerous subskills (Pink and Liebert 1986). Interestingly, some evidence indicates that skilled teachers are not as constrained by the curriculum as are novice teachers (Clark and Peterson 1986). Specifically, expert teachers do not begin thinking about instruction by thinking about the objectives. Instead, they typically plan instruction for large periods of time such as a school year, then organize their conceptualization into manageable units. Instructional planning for these smaller units consists largely of designing and organizing activities that they think will be effective. Then these activities are related to the objectives and tests.

Second, how the students are grouped in the school and in the classroom has enormous implications. Should students be grouped according to ability or grouped heterogeneously? Clearly this is a highly complex and controversial issue over which teachers often lack control. We take the position stated in *Becoming a Nation of Readers* (Anderson et al. 1985)—that it is important to group students heterogeneously. We believe that students of all ability levels may contribute to each other's learning in important ways. Moreover, when students are grouped homogeneously, either by tracking or ability grouping within the classroom, these groupings tend to become stable from one year to the next (Rist 1973), and negatively affect low-achieving students in terms of their self-concept and their achievement. This problem arises from many factors, including the stigma of being segregated, the tendency to set a pace that is often substantially less than challenging for such students, and a differential access to quality instruction (Levin 1986, Resnick and Resnick 1985).

Solutions to this problem are fraught with other difficulties. Of particular concern is the issue of limiting the learning opportunities for proficient students. Brophy (in progress) and Jones and Spady (1985) discuss various strategies for grouping and pacing that utilize heterogeneous grouping and yet seek to maximize learning opportunities for high-achieving students. Cooperative learning strategies seem particularly promising (e.g., Slavin, Sharon, Kagan, Hertz-Lazarowitz, Webb, and Schmuck 1984). We would also refer the reader to the strategy for low-achieving students developed by Alvermann (this volume).

*   *   *

To summarize, in this chapter we have presented a framework for teaching that has emerged from cognitive science and research on expert teaching. The overarching concept of this chapter, to which all the other concepts relate, is strategic teaching. In presenting this framework, we have attempted (1) to define the role of the teacher as thinker and decision maker, as content expert, and as model and mediator; (2) to provide a philosophy about teaching that focuses on teaching thinking in the content areas, and (3) to identify the various factors that skilled teachers think about during planning and teaching.

From the outset, strategic teachers are aware of constraints imposed by the context, and they develop strategies for coping with them to maximize quality of instruction. Strategic teachers are also skilled at aligning the variables of instruction (the learner, the instructional materials, the criterial task, and teaching/learning strategies) and assessment into a dynamic interaction that leads to acquisition of knowledge and conceptual change.

In addition, strategic teachers are sensitive to the process of learning. Especially important is their focus on helping students construct meaning and become aware of their own thinking as they undertake school tasks. In this effort, strategic teachers have the dual agenda of attending to both the nature of the content and to the teaching/learning strategies that will enhance learning the content and lead to student independence with flexible responses to different learning contexts. Some of these strategies focus on helping students link prior and new information as they are learning; still other teaching/learning strategies help students consolidate, integrate, and extend what they know.

Another theme of this chapter is the focus on developing effective instructional strategies that are designed to promote independent learning. Specifically, our definition of explicit strategy instruction includes assessing what strategies the students currently use, explaining new strategies, modeling them, scaffolding the instruction to permit gradual release of teacher support, and, where possible, providing opportunities for applying these ideas to new situations.

Finally, we considered various ways for teachers to assess both content and strategies. Informally constructed measures for classroom use should have instructional value, and they should be aligned with the objectives and the level of learning expected as well as with the substance of instruction.

We conclude by pointing out the many parallels between strategic teaching and learning. Just as strategic learning is planful and effortful, so, too, strategic teaching involves planning and effort to orchestrate the variables of instruction to relate harmoniously to and flow dynamically through each phase of learning. Both strategic learning and strategic teaching involve developing a repertoire of cognitive and metacognitive strategies upon which to draw to acquire and produce information, to solve problems, and to monitor the process of learning. Just as the strategic learner thinks carefully about selecting a learning strategy that is appropriate to the content and task, so, too, the strategic teacher conceptualizes teaching/learning strategies as a *means* of learning in particular contexts. Lastly, both strategic learning and teaching occur in phases, yet have elements that are nonlinear and recursive. Thus, lesson planning and teaching, like learning, is a constructive thinking process that involves preparation, intense interaction with the content, and integration and application of what is learned.

Planning Guide 3
Thinking Processes

Thinking Processes	Instructional Strategies
PREPARATION FOR LEARNING	**PREPARATION FOR LEARNING**
Comprehend objective/task	*Discuss objective/task*
define learning objectives	discuss/define nature of task
consider task/audience	discuss audience/learning goals
determine criteria for success	model/elicit criteria for success
Preview/Select materials/cues at hand	*Preview/Select materials/cues at hand*
skim features, graphic aids	model/guide previewing of materials
determine content focus/organizational pattern	elicit content focus/organizational pattern
Activate prior knowledge	*Activate/Provide background knowledge*
access content and vocabulary	elicit/provide content and vocabulary
access categories and structure	confront misconceptions, discuss strategies
access strategies/plans	elicit/provide categories and structural pattern
Focus interest/Set purpose	*Focus interest/Set purpose*
form hypotheses and questions/make predictions	brainstorm, model/guide hypotheses and predictions
represent/organize ideas (categorize/outline)	model/guide formulating questions for meaning
ON-LINE PROCESSING (Text Segments)	**PRESENTATION OF CONTENT**
Modify Hypotheses/Clarify ideas	*Pause and reflect/Discuss (after segments)*
check hypotheses, predictions, questions	model/guide checking predictions, etc.
compare to prior knowledge	model/guide comparing to prior knowledge
ask clarification questions	model/guide asking clarification questions
examine logic of argument, flow of ideas	elicit/discuss faulty logic/contradictions/gaps
generate new questions	model/guide raising issues/formulating questions
Integrate ideas	*Integrate ideas (after segments)*
select important concepts/words	brainstorm, model/guide reasoning for selection
connect and organize ideas, summarize	model/guide summarizing text segments
Assimilate new ideas	*Assimilate new ideas (after segments)*
articulate changes in knowledge	brainstorm, model/guide articulation
evaluate ideas/products	provide conferences/feedback, correctives
withhold judgment	discuss reasons for withholding judgment
CONSOLIDATING/EXTENDING ("The Big Picture")	**APPLICATION AND INTEGRATION**
Integrate/organize meaning for whole	*Integrate/organize meaning for whole*
categorize and integrate information, conclude	brainstorm key ideas, find categories/patterns
summarize key ideas and connections	discuss organizational patterns/standards, model
evaluate/revise/edit	guide return to standards/evaluation process

Assess achievement of purpose/learning	*Assess achievement of purpose*
compare new learnings to prior knowledge	discuss "old" misconceptions/new learnings
identify gaps in learning and information	guide identification, diagnose/prescribe, coach
generate new questions/next steps	provide opportunities for questions and follow up
Extend learning	*Extend learning*
translate/apply to new situations	increase complexity/diversity of content and task
rehearse and study	discuss/guide mnemonics and indepth study skills

Adapted from *Thinking Skills Instruction in English/Language Arts,* Copyright © 1987. National Education Association.

References

Alvermann, D. E., L. C. Smith, and J. E. Readence. "Prior Knowledge Activation and the Comprehension of Compatible and Incompatible Text." *Reading Research Quarterly* 20, 4 (1985): 420-436.

Anderson, R. C., E. H. Hiebert, J. A. Scott, and I. A. G. Wilkinson. *Becoming a Nation of Readers: The Report of the Commission on Reading.* Urbana, Ill.: University of Illinois, Center for the Study of Reading, 1985.

Anderson, C. W., and E. L. Smith. "Teaching Science." In *The Educator's Handbook: A Research Perspective,* edited by V. Koehler. New York: Longman, Inc., 1987.

Armbruster, B. B., T. H. Anderson, and J. Ostertog. "Does Text Structure/Summarization Facilitate Learning from Text?" *Research Reading Quarterly* 22 (1987).

Bereiter, C., and M. Bird. "Identification and Teaching of Reading Strategies." *Cognition and Instruction* 2, 2 (1985): 131-156.

Bereiter, C., and M. Scardamalia. "Reconstruction of Cognitive Skills." Paper presented at the annual meeting of the American Educational Research Association, New Orleans, April 1984.

Berliner, D. C. "In Pursuit of the Expert Pedagogue." *Educational Research* 15 (April 1986): 5-14.

Borko, H., and J. A. Niles. "Description of Teacher Planning: Ideas for Teachers and Researchers." In *Educator's Handbook: A Research Perspective,* edited by V. Koehler. New York: Longman, 1986.

Borkowski, J. G., M. B. Johnston, and M. K. Reid. "Metacognition, Motivation, and the Transfer of Control Processes." In *Handbook of Cognitive, Social, and Neuropsychological Aspects of Learning Disabilities,* edited by S. J. Ceci. Hillsdale, N.J.: Erlbaum, 1986.

Bransford, J. D., R. Sherwood, N. Vye, and J. Rieser. "Teaching Thinking and Problem Solving." *American Psychologist* 41 (1986): 1078-1089.

Brophy, J. "Teachers' Strategies." Paper presented at the annual meeting of the American Educational Research Association, Washington, D.C., April 1987.

Brophy, J., and T. L. Good. "Teaching Behavior and Student Achievement." In *Handbook of Research on Teaching,* edited by M. C. Wittrock. New York: Macmillan, 1986.

Brown, A. L., J. D. Bransford, R. A. Ferrara, and J. C. Campione. "Learning, Remembering and Understanding." In *Handbook of Child Psychology, Vol. 3,* edited by J. Flavell and E. M. Markham. New York: Wiley, 1983.

Brown, A. L., and A. S. Palincsar. "Guided Cooperative Learning and Individual Knowledge Acquisition." To appear in *Cognition and Instruction: Issues and Agenda.* Hillsdale, N.J.: Erlbaum. In press.

Clark, C. M., and P. L. Peterson. "Teacher's Thought Processes." In *Handbook of Research on Teaching*, edited by M. C. Wittrock. New York: Macmillan, 1986.

Collins, A., J. S. Brown, and S. E. Newman. "Cognitive Apprenticeship: Teaching the Craft of Reading, Writing, and Mathematics." In *Cognition and Instruction: Issues and Agendas*, edited by L. B. Resnick. Hillsdale, N. J.: Erlbaum, in press.

Darch, C. B., D. W. Carnine, and E. J. Kameenui. "The Role of Graphic Organizers and Social Structure in Content Area Instruction." *Journal of Reading Behavior* xviii (1986): 275-295.

Duffy, G. G., L. R. Roehler, M. S. Meloth, L. G. Vavrus, C. Book, J. Putnam, and R. Wesselman. "The Relationship Between Explicit Verbal Explanations During Reading Skill Instruction and Student Awareness and Achievement: A Study of Reading Teacher Effects." *Reading Research Quarterly* 21, 3 (1986): 237-252.

Heimlich, J. E., and S. D. Pittleman. *Semantic Mapping: Classroom Applications*. Newark, Del.: International Reading Association, 1986.

Herber, H. L. "Developing Reading and Thinking Skills in Content Areas." In *Thinking and Learning Skills: Relating Instruction to Research, Vol. 1*, edited by J. W. Segal, S. F. Chipman, and R. Glaser. Hillsdale, N.J.: Erlbaum, 1985.

Holley, C. D., and D. F. Dansereau. *Spatial Learning Strategies: Techniques, Applications, and Related Issues*. New York: Academic Press, 1984.

Jenkins, J. R. "Four Points to Remember: A Tetrahedral Model of Memory Experiments." In *Levels of Processing and Human Memory*, edited by L. S. Cermak and F. I. M. Craik. Hillsdale, N.J.: Erlbaum, 1978.

Jones, B. F. "SPaRCS Procedures." In *Teaching Reading as Thinking*, edited by A. S. Palincsar, D. S. Ogle, B. F. Jones, and E. G. Carr. Alexandria, Va.: Association for Supervision and Curriculum Development, 1986.

Jones, B. F., M. R. Amiran, and M. Katims. "Teaching Cognitive Strategies and Text Structures Within Language Arts Programs." In *Thinking and Learning Skills: Relating Instruction to Research, Vol. 1*, edited by J. Segal, S. F. Chipman, and R. Glaser. Hillsdale, N.J.: Erlbaum, 1985.

Jones, B. F., and W. G. Spady. "Enhanced Mastery Learning and Quality of Instruction as Keys to Two Sigma Results in Schools." In *Improving Student Achievement Through Mastery Learning Programs*, edited by D. U. Levine. San Francisco: Jossey-Bass, 1985.

Jones, B. F., M. Tinzmann, L. B. Friedman, and B. J. Walker. *Teaching Thinking Skills in English/Language Arts*. Washington, D.C.: National Education Association, 1987.

Langer, J. "Examining Background Knowledge and Text Comprehension." *Reading Research Quarterly* 19 (1984): 468-481.

Levin, H. M. "Accelerated Schools for Disadvantaged Students." *Educational Leadership* 44 (1987): 19-21.

Marzano, R., R. Brandt, C. Hughes, B. F. Jones, B. Presseissen, S. Rankin, and C. Suhor. *Dimensions of Thinking*. Alexandria, Va.: Association for Supervision and Curriculum Development. In progress.

Ogle, D. S. "K-W-L Group Instruction Strategy." In *Teaching Reading as Thinking*, edited by A. S. Palincsar, D. S. Ogle, B. F. Jones, and E. G. Carr. Alexandria, Va.: Association for Supervision and Curriculum Development, 1986.

Palincsar, A. S., and A. L. Brown. "Interactive Teaching to Promote Independent Learning from Text." *The Reading Teacher* 39, 8 (1986): 771-777.

Paris, S. G., and E. Oka. "Self-Regulated Learning Among Exceptional Children." *Exceptional Children* 53, 2 (1986): 103-108.

Paris, S. G., and P. Winograd. "Metacognition in Academic Learning and Instruction." In *Dimensions of Thinking: Review of Research,* edited by B. F. Jones. Hillsdale, N.J.: Erlbaum. In progress.

Pink, W. T., and R. E. Liebert. *Reading Instruction in Elementary Schools: A Proposal for Reform.* 1986.

Pressley, M., and J. R. Levin, eds. *Cognitive Strategy Research: Educational Applications.* New York: Springer-Verlag, 1983.

Resnick, D. P., and L. B. Resnick. "Standards, Curriculum, and Performance: A Historical and Comparative Perspective." *Educational Researcher* 14 (1985): 5-21.

Rist, R. C. *The Urban School: A Factory for Failure.* Cambridge, Mass.: Institute of Technology Press, 1973.

Roheler, L. R., and G. G. Duffy. "Direct Explanation of Comprehension Processes." In *Comprehension Instruction: Perspectives and Suggestions,* edited by G. G. Duffy, L. R. Roehler, and J. Mason. New York: Longman, 1984.

Scardamalia, M., and C. Bereiter. "Teachability of Reflective Processes in Written Composition." *Cognitive Science* 8 (1984): 173-190.

Schoenfeld, A. H. *Mathematical Problem Solving.* New York: Academic Press, 1985.

Seligman, M. E. P. *Helplessness. On Depression, Development, and Death.* San Francisco: W. H. Freeman & Co., 1975.

Singer, H., and D. Donlan. *Reading and Learning from Text.* Hillsdale, N.J.: Erlbaum, 1985.

Slavin, R. E., S. Sharon, S. Kagan, R. Hertz-Lazerowitz, C. Webb, and R. Schmuck, eds. *Learning to Cooperate: Cooperating to Learn.* New York: Plenum, 1984.

Torgesen, J. K. "The Learning-Disabled Child as an Inactive Learner: Eductional Implications." In *Topics in Learning and Learning Disabilities* 2 (1982): 45-52.

Van Patten, J. R., C.-I. Chao, and C. M. Reigeluth. "A Review of Strategies for Sequencing and Synthesizing Information." *Review of Educational Research* 56 (1986): 437-472.

Weinstein, C. E., and R. F. Mayer. "The Teaching of Learning Strategies." In *Handbook of Research on Teaching,* edited by M. C. Wittrock. New York: Macmillan, 1986.

Weinstein, C. E., and V. L. Underwood. "Learning Strategies: The How of Learning." In *Relating Instruction to Research,* edited by J. Segal, S. Chipman, and R. Glaser. Hillsdale, N.J.: Erlbaum, 1985.

Wood, P., J. Bruner, and G. Ross. "The Role of Tutoring in Problem Solving." *Journal of Child Psychology and Psychiatry* 17 (1976): 89-100.

The Editors

3 Planning for Strategic Teaching: An Example

Because planning for strategic teaching is a critical issue, we wanted to provide an extended example that actually uses the planning guide and research presented in Chapter 2. Therefore, this entire chapter is devoted to a description of a teacher, Mrs. Sampson, as she plans for teaching a sequence on Andrew Jackson to her seventh-grade history class for the first time. This description is based on an actual preparation by one of the authors.

This "thinking aloud" description is rare in the research literature. As you read this example, note that while planning is a process, it is not a linear one. Like learning, teacher thinking cannot be reduced to a simple, step-by-step procedure. Note that Mrs. Sampson does not plan for just a single lesson. From the outset, she plans for a whole segment of instruction based on a conceptual whole: the presidency of Andrew Jackson. Note also the constant interplay of references to students' prior knowledge and attitudes as these factors relate to other considerations.

We hope that teachers and instructional leaders will be able to use this example as a model to aid in planning instruction, and that it will be useful to researchers and curriculum developers. At the same time, it is important to realize that this is only one example. Other examples in this book, such as those of Alvermann and Beach, demonstrate that applications of our framework can be, and must be, varied according to particular learning contexts.

Establishing Content Priorities

As she sat down to plan for this part of the unit, Mrs. Sampson knew she had allocated one week for it and intended to use both her class discussion and textbook reading to present the content. Her first step was to look through the textbook to analyze the content presented there. As she did, she noted that it identified Jackson as the president of the "common man." Three themes were presented: (1) the extension of voting rights to all white men, (2) the conflict with the "monster" (the National Bank of the U.S.), and (3) the conflict over the Tariff of 1828. Mrs. Sampson also noticed that the tariff issue was handled superficially and that she would have to expand on that herself by providing other materials for reading and by discussing it further in class to provide more background knowledge for the students.

Comment. Note that Mrs. Sampson not only identifies the key issues or content to be taught but also pauses to evaluate the textbook critically against her prior knowledge of the topic. Her decision to supplement the textbook with additional reading and class discussion addresses the problem of poorly written texts, a problem many teachers face.

Considering Organizational Patterns

As Mrs. Sampson reflected on the content in the section, she also considered how she would help students think about those issues presented. Would simply identifying and remembering them be useful? Would there be some way students could apply what they were learning to some other situations and make comparisons and contrasts? As Mrs. Sampson considered the issues Jackson faced, some parallels to current political problems seemed intriguing. What about addressing the ongoing concern over free trade and tariffs? That issue had been in the news this year. Why not compare and contrast Jackson's Kitchen Cabinet with Reagan's California Cabinet? Would students deal with the issue of formal vs. informal leadership in government? With the tensions between economists and the Federal Reserve Bank over the status of the American dollar in world markets, perhaps some contemporary parallels could be made. Issues Jackson faced were not unique to his time. By drawing some parallels to current issues, both the value of studying the problems and the attempts made to resolve them could be made more real to students, she thought. To help students get to that point, however, Mrs. Sampson knew that she would want to guide them in their identification of the problems and the process of attempting to resolve them. Therefore, first a problem/solution frame would be necessary for students' thinking, and then a comparison/contrast frame.

The comparison/contrast frame should be rather easy for the students, Mrs. Sampson thought, since they were fairly familiar with current issues and with the procedures for comparing and contrasting. However, the students had applied the problem/solution frames only once before in a social studies context; therefore she would have to plan for explicit strategy instruction. Specifically, she would model recalling the previous context to activate prior knowledge of the frame; then she would guide the students to apply the frame questions to this context, helping them make adjustments in the frame questions as needed.

Comment. Note that Mrs. Sampson has anticipated a potential problem of student learning, the need to guide students to identify the problems and issues faced in the Jackson presidency. Notice also how she conceptualizes the two organizational patterns (compare/contrast and problem/solution) as teaching/learning strategies (1) to help the students frame their thinking about Andrew Jackson, and (2) to help link the new information to prior knowledge.

At the same time, it is evident that Mrs. Sampson has assessed what strategies the students already have available to them. The students can use the compare/contrast strategy with relative independence, so she will not need to provide many supports. Because the problem/solution frame was still relatively new, she would have to guide the students to begin to use the strategy independently. Thus, although her guidance will provide some scaffolding, her long-term goal is to enable the students to use this frame independently.

Deciding on Outcomes

After considering the text materials and the knowledge she wanted students to gain as a result of the class efforts, Mrs. Sampson decided that she wanted her students to identify Jackson as a commoner and view his presidency as a time of expanded participation in government. Students should also remember what the three issues were that Jackson faced as president and how those issues are still contemporary in our government today, in different but related forms. Additionally, Mrs. Sampson wanted students to gain more confidence in their ability to think about problems and solutions and to make comparisons and contrasts between the problems of earlier eras and current problems. A culminating compare/contrast task should accomplish both the content and the strategy goals.

Comment. Notice how the outcomes relate to the dual agenda of the strategic teacher. Mrs. Sampson has selected a culminating task that integrates both the content and the organizational patterns that the students will use as learning strategies for comprehending the text. It is also important to note that because this assessment task requires in-depth processing, it will facilitate learning. Another feature of Mrs. Sampson's planning at this point is the alignment of objectives, content, learning strategies, and assessment.

Developing Instructional Strategies to Link Prior Knowledge

Next, Mrs. Sampson considered how she could present this material so that students would actively engage in the process of learning. She considered what the class already knew in order to provide links for the new knowledge. She also wondered what would help the students access their prior knowledge, thus motivating them to learn.

Because the class had just studied a unit on the expansion of America in the 1800s, Mrs. Sampson considered having the class brainstorm some of the conditions they thought would influence the presidents in the mid-1800s. She wondered, too, if any of the class knew something about Jackson: had they visited the Hermitage, heard the song about the Battle of New Orleans, read books on Jackson, or seen some television programs about him, given the fact that he is a colorful character in our history?

Mrs. Sampson knew many students would not have much background to draw on, and yet she wanted to frame their study so all could learn. She had been highlighting some individual features of the early presidents. She was trying to build for the students a way of differentiating and remembering presidents. She had led students to identify some particular characteristic of each president and to focus on key issues of his time. She wanted to continue this framework for thinking about presidents.

Comment. Having considered the level of students' prior knowledge, Mrs. Sampson is now ready to develop specific instructional strategies for linking the new information to that knowledge. Note also that the framework for understanding presidents is a continuation from previous instruction.

Checking Vocabulary and Text Features

Before making her decisions about how to teach the section on Jackson, Mrs. Sampson looked again at the material in the text to determine if there was any vocabulary that would need attention. She mused as she skimmed over the material, "Do students know what tariffs are? How will they build a meaning for nullification? Are they familiar with the concept of our money system—the use of bank notes and paper money?" She decided that she would need to develop a framework to help students understand these concepts as the study progressed.

Comment. In this segment of thinking, Mrs. Sampson considers systematically what the students do not know. Notice that she is highly selective in choosing vocabulary words for explicit instruction, selecting only words that are critical for understanding. Additionally, she plans to incorporate the various terms into a framework for thinking, thereby providing a vocabulary strategy that is context-rich.

Constructing an Instructional Plan

Preparing for learning. As she considered all of these factors, Mrs. Sampson decided to start the study of Jackson's era with a short brainstorming session of 5-10 minutes. This brainstorming would focus on facts about Jackson and any information the students had about the vocabulary terms she had selected. The brainstorming would be followed by having students complete an anticipation guide (Figure 3.1). She wrote statements that would help highlight the key issues she would develop. She wanted this to help set purposes for the study, and she decided to list the outcome objectives on the board as well. These were: (1) being able to describe Jackson, (2) discuss three issues Jackson faced and how they were resolved in the 1830s, and (3) compare and contrast those issues to their modern variations.

Figure 3.1. Anticipation Guide for Jackson

INDICATE WHETHER YOU THINK THE STATEMENTS ARE TRUE OR FALSE (T OR F). IF YOU ARE UNSURE, INDICATE BY USING A QUESTION MARK.

1. _____ His nickname was Stonewall.
2. _____ He was the hero of the Battle of New Orleans.
3. _____ People accused him of ruining the Bank of the U.S.
4. _____ He nearly destroyed the White House.
5. _____ Southerners hated his support of the tariffs placed on imports.
6. _____ Jackson was married to the wife of another man.
7. _____ He was famous for fighting the "monster."
8. _____ He was known as a Western commoner.

Developing the presentation. With the introduction planned, Mrs. Sampson then had to think about how to handle the development of the information. The section in the text was short. Could students read it independently? Should it be read in class with silent reading of short sections followed by discussion? Or should students fill in guided work sheets while they read silently and then discuss their responses? How could she integrate the discussion of vocabulary terms with the ideas she thought were important? Because she wanted to focus on the issues and their resolution, Mrs. Sampson decided to construct a guided frame for students to use as they read silently (Figure 3.2). The students would use this frame individually during their reading, and later the whole class would discuss their interpretations. Because the material was not particularly clear in the textbook, she also brought into class resource books to provide alternative perspectives and additional information about Jackson and his issues.

Applying and integrating. The final project would be for each student to select one of the three issues; read in current newspapers and magazines about

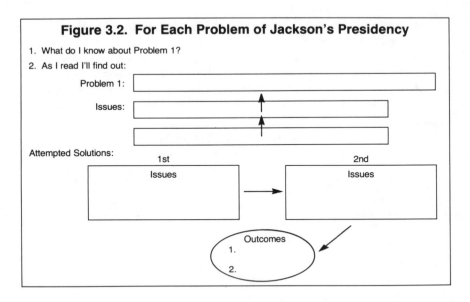

Figure 3.2. For Each Problem of Jackson's Presidency

1. What do I know about Problem 1?
2. As I read I'll find out:

Problem 1:

Issues:

Attempted Solutions:

1st Issues

2nd Issues

Outcomes
1.
2.

such an issue; and prepare a short paper comparing and contrasting Jackson's handling versus current handling of one of the issues discussed in the text. After the students had written the paper, she would guide them to assess what they had learned—both the content and the organizational strategies. Probably she would ask the students directly how they could evaluate what they learned. She would guide them to identify information about Jackson's presidency as well as to compare the problem/solution frame they used this time with the one they used before. She would also discuss with the class why the organizational patterns selected for this segment of instruction were appropriate.

Having engaged in this planning, Mrs. Sampson felt prepared and eager to begin the study of Jacksonian democracy. To help other teachers engage in the same thinking processes as Mrs. Sampson did, Figure 3.3 may prove useful as a work sheet.

Comment. Throughout the various phases of planning, Mrs. Sampson has integrated ideas of her own, ideas from Chapter 2, and items from Planning Guide 3 into a cohesive flow of instruction for a series of lessons forming a conceptual unit around Jackson's presidency.

What happens after planning? Probably Mrs. Sampson will not write out extensive lesson plans. Instead, she will jot down a few words and phrases that represent on paper what she has internalized as a brief "mental representation" or "notation" in terms of the three phases of instruction. Thus, what she actually writes down might look something like this:

- Preparation for learning → anticipation guide focusing on Jackson + a vocabulary framework;
- Presentation of content → explicit strategy instruction for problem/solution frame on problems and issues during Jackson's presidency; and
- Applying/integrating → written essay comparing and contrasting Jackson's presidency to the current presidency + assessment of learning.

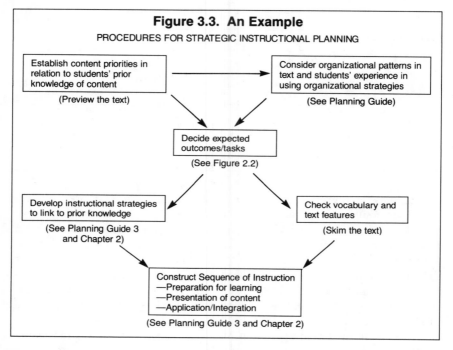

Figure 3.3. An Example

PROCEDURES FOR STRATEGIC INSTRUCTIONAL PLANNING

Establish content priorities in relation to students' prior knowledge of content

(Preview the text)

Consider organizational patterns in text and students' experience in using organizational strategies

(See Planning Guide)

Decide expected outcomes/tasks

(See Figure 2.2)

Develop instructional strategies to link to prior knowledge

(See Planning Guide 3 and Chapter 2)

Check vocabulary and text features

(Skim the text)

Construct Sequence of Instruction
—Preparation for learning
—Presentation of content
—Application/Integration

(See Planning Guide 3 and Chapter 2)

The specifics of the content and the instructional scaffolding that are fundamental to strategic teaching will flow automatically as Mrs. Sampson actually teaches this segment. Moreover, she knows that as she interacts with the students, she will modify and refine her plan to meet their needs and the demands of the particular learning context.

Part II

Applications to the Content Areas

Charles W. Anderson

Strategic Teaching in Science

his chapter discusses cognitive instruction in science; that is, teaching science in a way that helps students monitor and improve their thinking about the natural world. Much of this chapter is based on a program of research and development in which I and a number of colleagues (especially Edward L. Smith and Kathleen J. Roth) have been engaged for the last seven years. In this program, we have studied science teaching and learning at the elementary school, middle school, and college levels, and we have developed and implemented new approaches to teaching science at each level.

Our program is but a small part of a substantial research tradition involving researchers in many countries who have studied the teaching and learning of science from a cognitive perspective. This research tradition has produced books such as those by Driver, Guesne, and Tiberghien (1985) and by West and Pines (1985), as well as a variety of review articles such as those by Anderson and Smith (1987) and by Carey (1986).

In writing this chapter I was asked to address three questions:

1. To what extent is the framework for strategic teaching and learning that was developed in the first half of this book consistent with research in science?

2. To what extent is this framework helpful for planning sequences of instruction in my content area?

3. What adaptations, if any, need to be made to teach low- and high-achiev-

ing students so that all students will benefit from strategic teaching and cognitive instruction?

The chapter ends with direct answers to these questions. My answers are based on my understanding of the problems science teachers encounter in planning and in the classroom. Therefore the chapter begins with a discussion of those problems and of some of the solutions that we and others have developed. This discussion focuses on the problems encountered by a hypothetical teacher whom I shall call Ms. Lane.[1] She is a fifth-grade teacher who is preparing to teach a unit on light and vision. Although she is not familiar with the term "strategic learning," she shares many of its goals. In particular, she is concerned about her students' *understanding* of the content she teaches. She remembers science courses that she survived by memorizing for tests, then soon forgetting what she had memorized. Too often, she sees her students starting to do the same thing; they seem to come out of science lessons with memorized trivia rather than true understanding, and this is a matter of great concern to her.

Ms. Lane is dissatisfied when she sees her students memorizing rather than understanding, but what can she do to help them? This clearly is not an easy task; if it were, there would be a lot less memorizing in school science classes. In order to teach for understanding, Ms. Lane must develop solutions to a number of difficult problems. The following sections focus on four of those problems:

1. A definitional problem: What does it mean to "teach for understanding" in science?

2. A curricular problem: What is it about science that is worth understanding?

3. A student learning problem: How does scientific understanding develop in students?

4. An instructional problem: What can teachers do to help students understand?

---

[1]Although the episode described in this chapter is fictional, Ms. Lane is modeled on a real teacher, Dorothy Runyan, who has worked with us on research projects and teacher education programs for six years. She shares with us the concerns attributed to Ms. Lane, and she has experienced the problems we describe in teaching her fifth-grade students about light and vision, though not precisely in the form or the order described in this chapter. We owe a great debt to her and to the other elementary, middle school, and college teachers who have worked with us on our research and development program. The textbook described in the episode is also real: The *Green Book* in the Exploring Science Series (Blecha, Gega, and Green 1979). The criticisms we make of it also apply to most other science textbooks at all levels.

The Definitional Problem: Teaching for Understanding

Teaching for understanding is, of course, what this book is all about. Strategic teaching assumes that what teachers teach will be based in part on what they understand about how students learn. This focus on understanding is apparent in the six principles about learning with understanding that form the framework for Chapter 1 of this book. Restating these principles may aid science teachers like Ms. Lane to understand what it means to teach for understanding in science.

1. Learning is goal oriented; skilled learners are actively involved in constructing meaning and becoming independent learners.

2. Learning is linking new information to prior knowledge.

3. Learning is organizing knowledge.

4. Learning is strategic; skilled learners must develop a repertoire of effective learning strategies as well as be aware of and control their own activities.

5. Learning occurs in phases, yet is nonlinear and recursive; learners must think about what they already know, anticipate what they are to learn, assimilate new knowledge, and consolidate that knowledge.

6. Learning is influenced by development, and there are important developmental differences among learners.

learning

Ms. Lane is not an expert on educational research. She is, however, an experienced teacher who has developed her own ideas about understanding through years of practice. She is a good teacher, and as she compares her ideas with those listed above, she finds that they are highly compatible. (Unfortunately our research indicates that this is not universally true. Hollon and Anderson (1986), for example, found that some experienced teachers, typically teachers who do not understand science very well themselves, found the ideas above threatening and incompatible with their present practice.)

Therefore, Ms. Lane sets a goal for herself. She accepts the ideas listed above as a reasonable definition of learning with understanding, and she resolves to teach in a way that helps her students show these characteristics in their own learning. Before she can achieve this goal, however, she faces important problems involving curriculum, student learning, and instruction.

The Curricular Problem: What Is Worth Knowing?

At the outset of curriculum planning, Ms. Lane and other science teachers must decide what they want their students to learn. It seems reasonable to expect that textbooks are not as helpful in this respect as they should be. When Ms. Lane opens her textbook to the unit on light, she discovers that the textbook presents only a deceptive appearance of having clearly defined "content" that can be taught to students in a straightforward manner. In fact, she can interpret the textbook from a variety of different perspectives, and each perspective suggests a different definition of the curricular content of the light unit. Three perspectives that are common among teachers and science educators are contrasted below.

Teaching Science as Facts, Rules, and Definitions

When she looks at her textbook, the first thing that Ms. Lane notices is that it contains a lot of facts (light travels in straight lines; light travels very fast; the colors in the spectrum . . .). There are also some definitions (transparent, translucent, opaque, lens, retina . . .). Although this textbook does not have them, it is also common for more advanced texts to contain formulas and rules. It certainly seems reasonable, looking at a science textbook, to think of science as a long list of facts, rules, and definitions to be learned. The most reasonable interpretation of Ms. Lane's textbook is certainly that the authors intended science to be taught this way.

Writing textbooks that present lots of facts makes good business sense. This way of thinking about science is common among the teachers we have worked with in our research and development projects (Anderson and Smith in press, Hollon and Anderson 1986). Even college professors often treat science teaching essentially as the presentation of facts, rules, and definitions, albeit in a well-structured and organized manner (Anderson 1986). Thus teaching science by presenting facts, rules, and definitions represents the "path of least resistance" for both teachers and textbook publishers.

Unfortunately, it is virtually impossible to teach lists of facts in the meaningful way that we defined as cognitive instruction at the beginning of this chapter. Learning facts puts the students in a passive rather than an active role, encourages memorization rather than the active construction of knowledge, and fails to connect science content with students' prior knowledge of the world. Because of these deficiencies, attempts to teach science as facts, rules, and definitions typically produce little understanding and less retention (cf. Anderson, Sheldon, and DuBay forthcoming; Anderson and Smith in press; Clement 1982). Ms. Lane knows from experience that she needs to do more than teach her students lists of facts, rules, and definitions. There *must* be more to science than that, but what?

Teaching Science as Process Skills

One popular answer to Ms. Lane's question focuses on "science process skills." These are the skills necessary to conduct investigations of the natural world, such as observing, measuring, inferring, and so forth. When Ms. Lane looks at her textbook, she sees that in addition to facts and definitions it has "finding out" activities. Although the activities in this book are not particularly good, it would be possible to modify these experiences and use them to provide students with hands-on laboratory activities that would provide training and practice in science process skills. Would this be enough to help Ms. Lane's students learn science with understanding?

Unfortunately, the research evidence suggests that hands-on activities or instruction in process skills will not ensure meaningful learning, either alone or in combination with conventional fact-based instruction (Roth 1984, Smith and Anderson 1984). One problem is that science processes do not seem to consist of unitary skills that can be transferred from one context to another. Observing cell cultures, for example, has little in common with observing geological formations or with observing chemical reactions. Furthermore, a major component of process skills seems to be content knowledge (e.g., a good observer of cell cultures must know a lot about cells).

So science is more than the sum of process skills plus facts, rules, and definitions. Ms. Lane must find a different way of thinking about the content that she teaches before she can truly engage in cognitive instruction in science.

Teaching Science as Explanation

There is another approach to defining the content of science, one that has much more potential for serving as the basis for cognitive instruction in science. This approach emphasizes the explanatory functions of science. Science is our best attempt to explain *how* and *why* events happen as they do in the natural world. How does light help us to see, for example? How do we see colors? Why do plants need light to grow? Why is the sky blue?

If Ms. Lane looks hard, she can find passages in her textbook in which scientific principles are used to explain natural phenomena. Here, for instance, is a passage explaining how light helps us to see:

Like a rubber ball, light bounces off most things it hits. When light travels to something opaque, all the light does not stop. Some of this light bounces off. When light travels to something translucent or transparent, all the light does not pass through. Some of this light bounces off. When light bounces off things and travels to your eyes, you are able to see (Blecha, Gega, and Green 1979, p. 154).

Is this a "main point" of the unit on light? There is certainly no indication that the authors of the text thought of it that way. The passage quoted above is buried in the middle of a chapter; no special markers indicate its importance. Our research, though, has convinced us that Ms. Lane and other science teachers can truly teach for understanding only if they "reconstruct" the contents of science texts, putting much more emphasis than most texts do on using scientific theories and principles to explain phenomena in the natural world.

77

There are a number of advantages to focusing on science as explanation. This approach gives back to scientific theories their original purpose, a purpose that all too often is lost in science as it is taught in schools. Scientists develop their theories because they have *questions* about how and why the world works. All too often, we teach students the answers (or procedures for getting answers) without letting them know what the questions are. Recent work in the history and philosophy of science has emphasized that science is fundamentally an attempt to describe and explain the natural world. Scientific progress involves constructing more powerful descriptions and explorations, not simply discovering more facts and laws according to the "scientific method" (cf. Kuhn 1970, Mayr 1982, Toulmin 1961).

So Ms. Lane decides that she will emphasize the explanatory functions of science in her treatment of the light unit. She will ask questions calling for explanations and help her students use passages from the text like the one above to construct scientific answers to those questions. In making this decision, Ms. Lane has taken an important step toward cognitive instruction in science. She has decided to involve her students in a central activity of science, one that requires them to actively construct meaning and to organize and use their personal and scientific knowledge. She has also taken a key step toward linking the information in the light unit to her students' prior knowledge. This linkage is examined in detail in the next section.

The Student Learning Problem: How Does Scientific Understanding Develop?

Ms. Lane has now made a strategic curricular decision about her unit on light and vision: she will emphasize teaching her students to explain phenomena scientifically. As she looks through the textbook, she can now see a number of phenomena that she wants her students to explain: how we see; how light interacts with transparent, translucent, and opaque objects; how our eyes work; and so forth. She cannot mediate learning successfully, however, until she understands what her students will be going through as they try to master the key scientific principles and use them to construct explanations. There are two aspects to this understanding: (1) the nature of students' prior knowledge and how it must change, and (2) the strategies that students use for processing new information about science.

Students' Prior Knowledge and the Process of Conceptual Change

Explanations provide a link between science content and students' prior knowledge when facts do not. Students generally just do not know scientific facts before they begin a new unit, so if science is defined as consisting of facts, rules, and definitions, it often appears that students simply know nothing about the topic they are to study. A different and more complex picture emerges, however, if students are asked to explain things that they see in the world around them. It turns out that students *do* have explanations, but not the ones that scientists have developed. A look at the nature of students' explanations reveals why learning science is so complex and difficult for most students.

Consider, for example, the explanation quoted above from Ms. Lane's textbook about how light helps us to see objects. What do students say if they are asked how light helps us to see things? We asked this question to large numbers of fifth graders (Anderson and Smith 1987; Eaton, Anderson, and Smith 1984), and the following are typical answers:

"In the dark, you can't see anything, so it makes things so you can see them."

"It brightens the path to the object we are looking at."

"It lights up the object so you can see it."

These student explanations certainly are not untrue or unreasonable, but they do not seem entirely satisfactory, either. What is missing (aside from some fancy vocabulary) in these explanations that is present in the textbook explanation quoted above? You might want to take a minute to compare the text and student explanations for yourself before reading on.

*   *   *

There are actually several problems with the student explanations. The first one, for instance, is not really an explanation at all; it restates the question in different words. Perhaps the most important thing to notice about these explanations—a characteristic that shows up over and over whenever students discuss vision—is that they *do not mention reflected light*. In our investigations of students' ideas about how we see, we have found that only about 5 percent of the fifth graders we studied were aware that reflected light played a role in vision. The rest thought that light merely made things bright or visible so that we could see them directly.

Our investigations of students' conceptions of light and vision revealed that students' explanations of common phenomena differed from scientific explanations in many other ways as well. Students generally believed that their eyes worked by seeing objects rather than by detecting light, for example. Many students were not sure whether light was always in motion or not. Most students thought that white light was clear or colorless, rather than a combination of the colors of the spectrum. We discovered that students had an interconnected network of mutually supporting beliefs about light and vision that made sense to them, but that were incompatible with the scientific ideas presented in the textbook.

The books and review articles cited at the beginning of this chapter describe similar student beliefs about dozens of other scientific topics. These student beliefs are incompatible with scientific theories; for this reason we label them *misconceptions*. They are not, however, foolish or completely wrong. They are often compatible with our normal language. (For example, we generally say, "I look out the window and see the tree," rather than, "I see the light reflected by the tree coming in the window to my eyes.") Misconceptions are generally ideas that are reasonable and appropriate in a limited context, but students inappropriately apply them to situations where they do not work.

A strategic teacher in science must understand the dual nature of students' prior scientific knowledge. In part, prior knowledge is the foundation for meaningful learning in science. Students must relate scientific theories to their own ideas about the world in order to see science as a means of understanding the world rather than a collection of arcane and disconnected facts. On the other hand, students' misconceptions are barriers to successful learning. They must give up or modify many of their beliefs about the world in order to truly understand science.

Thus, science learning is a complex process of *conceptual change*, in which students must modify some of their beliefs about how the world works while strengthening and reorganizing others. In this way, successful learners of science gradually reconstruct their understanding of the natural world. The interconnected and mutually supporting nature of student misconceptions makes this process an arduous one for most students.

Students' Science Learning Strategies

Ms. Lane thinks about the process of conceptual change, and it helps her understand why she was so concerned about her students' learning. They were not really going through the process of conceptual change. They were just memorizing a few facts without altering their misconceptions at all! Still, she is puzzled. She can find many passages in the book like the one about vision quoted earlier. How could students *read* those passages without seeing the conflict?

My colleague Kathleen Roth has conducted a study that helps to answer Ms. Lane's question (Roth 1985). She conducted careful analyses of students' thinking as they read science textbooks. The students in her study were middle school students reading chapters from one of three texts, two commercial and one experimental, about photosynthesis, the process by which plants use sunlight to make their own food.

In order to truly understand these textbooks, the students in Roth's study had to go through a process of conceptual change. All the students in the study began with a number of important misconceptions, including the belief that plants get their food from the soil rather than making it themselves. She found, however, that most students did not change their basic ideas about food for plants. Instead, they relied on reading strategies that enabled them to cope with the normal demands of school through superficial learning rather than true conceptual change. Roth described at least five different strategies or approaches to reading science textbooks, only one of which resulted in conceptual change. Those five strategies are described below (from Roth 1985).

1. Overreliance on prior knowledge in order to complete a school task. Students using this strategy were generally below-grade-level readers who interpreted the text almost completely in terms of their prior knowledge and incorrect beliefs about plants and food. When asked to recall what the text said, for example, they frequently attributed to the text things that were not in the text but came from their prior knowledge. Although they reported the text made sense to them, these students appeared to avoid thinking about the text itself as much as possible. If they could decode the words and get enough of the gist of the text to call up some appropriate prior knowledge, they reported that the text "made sense."

For example, Maria read a section of the *Concepts in Science* (Brandwein et al. 1980) text that used milk as an example of how all food can ultimately be traced back to green plants, the food producers. Maria announced that "most of this stuff I already knew," and that this was the easiest section to understand. "It was about milk." When probed, she expanded her summary of the text: "It's just about milk . . . how we get our milk from cows." She never picked up any notion that plants make food. This is typical of her pattern of reading to find similar ideas, ignoring the rest of the text and relying on prior knowledge to fill in the details.

The students using this strategy answered questions posed in the text by thinking about their real-world knowledge about plants rather than using text knowledge. Without thinking about plants' roles in producing food, for example, Maria came up with the right answer to the following question by thinking about her prior knowledge:

Question: All the food we eat can be traced finally back to the
(a) green plants
(b) cows

Maria correctly picked (a) and explained: "I don't know . . . I just circled green plants because everybody eats . . . not everybody eats cows but *everybody* eats green plants."

Thus strategy 1 enabled students to complete assigned tasks and comply with school expectations without really engaging the text at all.

2. Overreliance on words in the text in order to complete a school task. Another group of students, also generally poor readers, isolated words without relating those words to each other or to any prior real-world knowledge. In recalling what they had read, these students identified words or phrases ("It was about chlor-something and an ecosystem") without giving any description or meaning to them. In spite of this lack of attention to meaning, these students reported that they "understood" the text if they were able to decode the words and to identify details in the text that satisfactorily answered questions posed by the text. They reported feeling confused only when they encountered unfamiliar words that they could not decode. For example, when asked whether there were any places in the *Modern Science* text (Smith, Blecha, and Pless 1974) that were confusing, Tracey reported that it was just "some of the words I didn't get." On day three, she pointed out the following *words* as places where she was confused: fermentation, chlorophyll, chloroplast, cotyledon, embryo, dormant.

In answering text-posed questions, students using this strategy simply looked for a "big" word in the question, located that word in the text, and copied the word along with words surrounding it in the text. These copied words may or may not have sensibly answered the question, but the students were satisfied just to have an answer. Frequently, this strategy produced answers that would be acceptable to most teachers. When students were asked interview questions about real-world plants, students relied totally on their experience and prior knowledge. They saw no relationship between the text and the plants. Thus, Tracey recalled the book being about "chlorophyll" and "photosynthesis," but these words were never mentioned when she was asked about how a particular plant gets its food.

The students' use of the text was driven by their school knowledge of what was needed to finish the work. They had found that being able to recite key words and phrases from the text (especially large vocabulary words) can often get you by. Real-world knowledge was for them a completely separate realm of knowledge used to explain everyday, nontext phenomena.

3. Overreliance on unrelated facts in the text due to an "addition" notion of learning. This strategy was used by better readers who tried to learn from the text instead of just trying to finish the assigned work. These students held the view that school science learning is all about developing lists of facts about natural phenomena. Their prior experience with schooling had convinced them that memorization of unrelated facts is satisfactory learning. They rarely attempted to relate the facts from the text to each other or to their real-world knowledge about plants.

Students using this strategy often had fairly accurate and complete recall of explicit text material. However, they remembered ideas in no particular conceptual order, they placed equal emphasis on trivial details and on main concepts, and they did not link facts together to develop an overall picture of the main concepts. For example, Myra remembered a lot of details about an experiment that had been described in the *Concepts in Science* text:

She had some fish and she had some plants in there and one day she was looking at them and a bubble came out of one of the plants. And she started experimenting a little, and she noticed they were giving off oxygen. . . . They asked us what we think about what is she trying—is it oxygen, they asked us what we thought. I put one time it did and one time it didn't. . . . They said the first time it wasn't sunny all the time. The first time it was out for one week and every day it was sunny.

However, when the interviewer asked Myra whether the girl doing the experiment had made a conclusion about the role of the sun, Myra said simply, "no." Although she remembered a lot of details, she missed the critical reason for including the experiment in the text.

Like students using the first two strategies, students using this strategy answered questions about real plants without making reference to any of the facts they had read about in the text and included in their recall. Since they separated school science from plants in the real world, they could not use information in the text to change their misconceptions about food for plants. Thus the text failed to help them through the process of conceptual change.

4. Overreliance on prior knowledge in order to make sense of disciplinary/text knowledge. This strategy was used by a relatively large number of students, most of whom were reading at or above grade level as measured by standardized achievement tests. These students did not focus primarily on developing strategies to get by in school. Instead, they seemed to be genuinely trying to make sense of the text and the disciplinary knowledge it contained. Thus, in contrast with the first three strategies, this is a sophisticated strategy in which readers attempted to link prior knowledge and text knowledge. These students generally expected the text to *confirm* their prior knowledge, however, so that their goal in reading the text was basically to verify and add details to what they already knew. This attitude was expressed by some as, "Basically, I already knew all this."

Because the students' prior knowledge was so strongly held and because it was often in conflict with the text content, the students using this strategy had to distort or ignore some of the text information to make it fit. Thus, these students *did* integrate prior knowledge and disciplinary knowledge. However, with prior knowledge taking the driver's seat in the process, learning was often quite different from what was intended by the authors of the text.

   5. Conceptual change strategy. Some students in Roth's study, all but one of whom were reading the experimental text, used a conceptual change reading strategy. These students also worked to reconcile text information with their prior knowledge, but they allowed the text to take the driver's seat in their attempts to integrate real-world knowledge and text knowledge. Thus, they used text knowledge to *change* their ideas about food for real plants. These students recognized the conflicts between what the text was saying and their own naive theories, and this conflict was resolved by abandoning or changing their misconceptions in favor of the more powerful, sensible disciplinary explanation.

   All of the students using this strategy displayed abilities as they read the texts that were not observed among the other students, including the following:

   (a) They could recognize and state the main concepts of the text.

   (b) They were aware of the *conflict* between text explanations and their misconceptions and willing to abandon misconceptions to resolve the conflict.

   (c) They were aware that the text was leading to changes in their own thinking about real-world knowledge.

   (d) They were aware of places where the text explanations were confusing because they were in conflict with their previous beliefs.

   (e) They could use text ideas to answer questions about real plants.

   The students using the conceptual change strategy found it to be hard work; they were the *most* likely to acknowledge feeling confused or having difficulty understanding the text. All of the other strategies left the students feeling confident that they had "understood" because they never really recognized the differences between the text's view of how plants get their food and their own naive views. All of the reading strategies "worked" in the sense that they helped students get through school tasks, but only the conceptual change strategy truly leads to learning with understanding.

Implications of Research on Student Learning

   As Ms. Lane looks at her text she begins to see why most of her students do not understand it very well. The text does contain some useful explanations, but it does not really challenge students to think about or change their own explanations. It uses boldface type to emphasize new words, not important ideas. The "main ideas" listed for each chapter are generally facts. The questions in the book and the unit test can be answered from students' prior knowledge or through factual recall. No wonder students generally use ineffective strategies when they read science texts!

   Ms. Lane, though, does not just want to explain her students' difficulties. She wants to help them understand science. What can she do? It would be nice if she could get a better text. (In Roth's study, the conceptual change reading strategy was used by six of the seven students reading the experimental text, but by only one of the 12 students using the two commercial texts, a seventh grader reading at the twelfth-grade level.)

Like most teachers, however, Ms. Lane is stuck with the text she has. What can she do in her classroom to make cognitive instruction a reality? How can she, as a teacher, help her students engage in conceptual change learning? These are instructional questions, and they are addressed in the next section.

The Instructional Problem: Helping Students Understand

This section summarizes research findings about some of the key elements of a teaching strategy that leads to conceptual change in students. The research on which this section is based includes work by Minstrell (1984) and Nussbaum and Novick (1982) as well as our own research (e.g., Roth, Anderson, and Smith forthcoming). The research is built on comparisons between teaching that does lead to conceptual change in most students with teaching of similar materials under similar circumstances that does not. Thus, the techniques recommended here have been used successfully by classroom teachers (including Ms. Lane). This research is reviewed in Anderson and Smith (1987).

Teaching for conceptual change can be described as a three-stage process. First, there is a *preparation* phase, in which students begin to think about the phenomena that will be explained in the unit, discuss their own explanations, and become aware of the limitations of their naive explanations. Second, there is a *presentation* phase, in which teachers explain key scientific principles and theories. Finally, there is a phase of *application and integration*, in which students apply the scientific principles to new phenomena and integrate those principles and theories into their personal and scientific knowledge. These three phases are summarized in the Planning Guide for Teaching for Conceptual Change at the end of this chapter and are discussed below.

Preparation for Conceptual Change

Students generally begin learning about a topic with, at best, a vague sense that they could learn more than they now know. They generally expect that learning to consist of facts, rules, and definitions, and they generally begin with few unanswered questions about the topic. They seldom have really noticed and observed the phenomena associated with that topic. Many of Ms. Lane's students, for example, have never noticed where they have to stand to see someone else in a mirror or what a pencil looks like in a glass of water. They have never asked themselves where the colors of the rainbow come from or which direction light is traveling when they "look out" of a window. If students are to engage successfully in the active, difficult work of conceptual change learning, they need a sense of what the *potential* is for their learning, of what it is they don't know about the topic but would like to find out.

A variety of instructional techniques can help students become aware of potential learning and develop personally owned questions that will drive active inquiry into a topic. Simple advance organizers that provide a conceptual overview of what students will learn are often useful. It is also important to get students engaged in observing and talking about the phenomena that the unit will focus on. Encouraging observation of discrepant events, where students see things happen that their own conceptions do not lead them to expect, is useful. It is also useful to promote careful observation and thinking about everyday events or objects that play a significant role in students' daily lives, especially if you can ask provocative questions that will lead students to question how well they understand those objects and events. Dialogue and debate among students can help them become aware of other ways than their own to think about the objects and events that they are observing. All of these techniques help students become actively engaged with the content of the unit.

Teachers can also learn a great deal from these initial discussions. By listening to students' explanations and ideas, they can begin to gain some insight into their students' prior knowledge and misconceptions. These insights will be of great use to them as they continue teaching the unit.

Introduction of Scientific Concepts

While such exploratory activities are useful, they do not in themselves lead to conceptual change learning (cf. Smith and Anderson 1984). Left to their own devices, students may discover many interesting things about plants or light, but they will develop scientific ideas about photosynthesis or vision about as rapidly as the human race: in other words, not in a single lifetime.

Therefore, scientific concepts need to be explicitly introduced and taught to students. Students must see the scientific concepts as important, meaningful, and comprehensible. They must understand that the scientific concepts are different from their own previous ideas, but not so strange or difficult that they cannot be understood.

We have found that students comprehend scientific concepts better when they are introduced in the context of a meaningful problem, not simply as facts or definitions to be learned. Thus, for example, the previously quoted passage in Ms. Lane's text explaining how we see will be more meaningful to students if they have been discussing that question before reading the passage.

Contrasting scientific concepts and common student misconceptions is also useful. Ms. Lane, for instance, can help her students by clearly pointing out that their explanations of how we see do not mention reflected light, but the book does; or she can help them understand that looking out of a window is actually detecting light coming *in*.

Finally, it is important to emphasize key concepts through such devices as repetition and highlighting (using bold print and putting key concepts in boxes). This may seem like obvious advice, but look at what is emphasized in a typical science textbook: the vocabulary words!

Application and Integration

Research on learning indicates that students initially learn new concepts in specific task contexts and often have difficulty transferring what they have learned to other contexts. This is true even if the concepts are in fact broadly and generally applicable. Thus students cannot fully master a new concept or appreciate its significance until they have successfully used it in a variety of different contexts.

Therefore each important concept should be included in a variety of different tasks, and its presence and importance should be explicitly signaled. For example, the idea that seeing is detecting reflected light can be used to explain why we cannot see through walls (do they block our "view" or the light coming toward us from the other side?), how our eyes work, how we see colors, why frosted glass makes things look blurry, and so forth. Only when students have successfully explained these and other situations can they truly be said to understand that we see by detecting reflected light.

Discussion of Instructional Strategies

One useful way of bringing together the teaching strategies discussed above is to consider a science classroom as a *learning community*. An ideal community for the learning of science needs to be different from a typical science classroom. Students should be actively engaged not just in learning facts and practicing skills, but in practicing the activities of scientifically literate adults: explanation, description, prediction, and control of objects and events in the natural world. Students in such an ideal learning community learn science from sources of *authority* such as textbooks and the teacher, from *evidence* that they acquire by working with natural objects and events, and from *communication* with each other and their teacher.

Creating such an ideal learning community in an ordinary classroom is not an easy task. Textbooks and other teaching materials are generally designed to support memorization and skill practice, not the understanding of science. Young children are typically curious about the world, but they are not naturally disciplined learners of science. Older students often habitually use learning strategies that help them get through science classes, but that does not lead to true scientific understanding. Teachers often work under conditions that do not encourage the creation of ideal learning communities. Nevertheless, we have seen Ms. Lane and other teachers use teaching strategies like those described above to create true (if not ideal) learning communities in their classrooms. They are truly engaged in cognitive instruction in science.

Conclusion

In discussing the problems that Ms. Lane and other teachers encounter in planning and teaching science, I have implicitly answered the questions posed at the beginning of the chapter. This concluding section makes those answers more explicit.

1. *Is the framework for strategic teaching and learning developed in the first half of this book consistent with research in science?* Yes, it is. I have tried to show in this chapter how successful learning and instruction in science has each of the characteristics of successful learning and instruction discussed in Part I of this book. Moreover, I have tried to portray strategic teaching in science as a complex and demanding enterprise. It is hard work, and it demands an understanding of science content, of students and their scientific thinking, and of appropriate teaching strategies. There are at least three ways in which we can work to help science teachers become more successful at strategic teaching in science.

First, we can improve science textbooks and other teaching materials. Roth and others have demonstrated in their research that it is possible to write textbooks that lead to much higher levels of student understanding than current commercial textbooks. Commercial publishers, however, produce what the market demands, which is currently broad content coverage, lots of facts, and lots of features. The true impetus for improvement in textbooks must come from the buyers, including members of the Association for Supervision and Curriculum Development.

Second, we can improve preservice and inservice teacher education to help teachers become aware of the issues discussed in this chapter, master cognitive instructional teaching strategies, and ask questions about their teaching that will lead to continued professional growth and development.

Finally, we can improve the conditions of teaching. Strategic teaching can become a widespread reality in the schools only if teachers have time for planning, grading, and professional growth, if they are rewarded for trying and using cognitive instructional strategies, and only if communities are formed in which teachers can help each other think about and try to improve their science teaching.

2. *To what extent is the framework developed in Part I of this book helpful for planning sequences of instruction in science?* I think it is very helpful, especially the generic planning guides: Planning Guide 1 for Thinking Processes and Planning Guide 3 for Strategic Teaching. The Planning Guide for Teaching for Conceptual Change that I developed for this chapter embodies the concepts in both generic guides. Specifically, the Planning Guide for Teaching for Conceptual Change conceptualizes science learning and instruction in terms of the three-phase process just like that used for other subjects, as well as particular teaching/learning strategies emphasized in Part I such as linking new information to prior knowledge.

3. *What adaptations, if any, need to be made to teach low- and high-achieving students so that all students will benefit from cognitive instruction?* I do not have a fully adequate answer to this question. In our studies we have expanded the percentage of students' understanding from the 0-20 percent range to the 50-80 percent range. This is clearly a great improvement, but we have yet to develop techniques that reach the lowest-achieving students. In particular, we suspect that we are not reaching (a) passive learners, (b) students who are frequently absent, (c) students who are learning-disabled or handicapped, and (d) students who are severely deficient in reading and writing skills.

I feel confident, however, that the path to improvement does not lie in special programs, particularly for low-achieving students. Instead, we need to find ways of creating classroom learning communities in which all students are full participants. Low-achieving students need very much to practice expressing their ideas, to listen to the ideas of others, and to have others listen to them.

This is one of many problems that I am still wondering about and working on as I look for better ways of teaching science. There is a sense in which strategic teaching and cognitive instruction in science are ideals that neither I nor any other science teacher can ever fully achieve. This chapter, however, describes many specific actions that teachers, administrators, and others can take to improve science teaching. Long-term improvements in science education will arise from the accumulation of those specific actions.

Planning Guide for Teaching for Conceptual Change

Student Thinking — *Teaching Strategies*

Preparation for Conceptual Change

Student Thinking	Teaching Strategies
Anticipate learning to take place	Provide advance organizers
Develop adequate descriptions of natural phenomena	Generate observation, discussion, and writing about everyday objects and events
Develop awareness of, and dissatisfaction with, own explanations	Question and debate explanations
	Generate observation and discussion of discrepant events

Introduction of Scientific Conceptions

Student Thinking	Teaching Strategies
Achieve initial minimal understanding of scientific explanations	Emphasize key principles and theories
Understand scientific conceptions as reasonable alternatives to own reasoning (not too difficult to understand, not just additions to their own ideas)	Contrast misconceptions and goal conceptions
	Introduce conceptions in the context of meaningful tasks

Application and Integration

Student Thinking	Teaching Strategies
Understand scientific principles and theories as widely applicable	Explicitly signaled inclusion of conceptions in other tasks, especially:
Understand interconnections with other personal and scientific ideas	—tasks in everyday contexts
	—tasks in other scientific contexts

References

Anderson, C. W. "Improving College Science Teaching: Problems of Conceptual Change and Instructors' Knowledge." Paper presented at the annual meeting of the National Association for Research in Science Teaching, San Francisco, 1986.

Anderson, C. W., T. H. Sheldon, and J. DuBay. "The Effects of Instruction on College Non-majors' Conceptions of Respiration and Photosynthesis." *Journal of Research in Science Thinking* (forthcoming).

Anderson, C. W., and E. L. Smith. "Teaching Science." In *The Educators' Handbook: A Research Perspective*, edited by V. Koehler. New York: Longman, 1987.

Blecha, M. K., P. C. Gega, and M. Green. *Green Book*. 2d ed. Exploring Science Series. River Forest, Ill.: Laidlaw, 1979.

Brandwein, P., E. Cooper, P. Blackwood, N. Cotton-Winslow, M. Giddings, F. Romero, and A. Carin. *Concepts in Science*. New York: Harcourt, Brace, Jovanovich, 1980.

Carey, S. "Cognitive Science and Science Education." *American Psychologist* 41, 10 (1986): 1123-1130.

Clement, J. "Students' Preconceptions in Introductory Physics." *American Journal of Physics* 50, 1 (1982): 66-71.

Driver, R., E. Guesne, and A. Tiberghien, eds. *Children's Ideas in Science*. Philadelphia: Open University Press, 1985.

Eaton, J. F., C. W. Anderson, and E. L. Smith. "Students' Misconceptions Interfere with Science Learning: Case Studies of Fifth-grade Students." *Elementary School Journal* 84, 4 (1984): 365-379.

Hollon, R. E., and C. W. Anderson. "Teachers' Understanding of Students' Scientific Thinking: Its Influence on Planning and Teaching." Paper presented at the annual meeting of the National Association for Research in Science Teaching, San Francisco, 1986.

Kuhn, S. *The Structure of Scientific Revolutions*. 2d ed. Chicago: University of Chicago Press, 1970.

Mayr, E. *The Growth of Biological Thought*. Cambridge, Mass.: Belknap, 1982.

Minstrell, James. "Teaching for the Development of Understanding of Ideas. Forces on Moving Objects." In *Observing Science Classroom: Perspectives from Research and Practice*, 1984 Yearbook of the Association for the Education of Teachers in Science, edited by C. W. Anderson. Columbus, Ohio: ERIC/SMEAC, 1984.

Nussbaum, J., and S. Novick. "Alternative Frameworks, Conceptual Conflict, and Accommodation: Toward a Principled Teaching Strategy." *Instructional Science* 11, 3 (1982): 183-200.

Roth, K. J. "Using Classroom Observations to Improve Science Teaching and Curriculum Materials." In *Observing Science Classrooms: Perspectives from Research and Practice*, 1984 Yearbook of the Association for the Education of Teachers in Science, edited by C. W. Anderson. Columbus, Ohio: ERIC/SMEAC, 1984.

Roth, K. J. "Conceptual Change Learning and Student Processing of Science Texts." Paper presented at the annual meeting of the American Educational Research Association, Chicago, 1985.

Roth, K. J., C. W. Anderson, and E. L. Smith. "Curriculum Materials, Teacher Talk, and Student Learning: Case Studies of Fifth-Grade Science Teaching." *Journal of Curriculum Studies* (forthcoming).

Smith, E. L., and C. W. Anderson. "Plants as Producers: A Case Study of Elementary Science Teaching." *Journal of Research in Science Teaching* 21 (1984): 685-698.

Smith, H. A., M. K. Blecha, and H. Pless. *Modern Science, Level Six*. River Forest, Ill.: Laidlaw, 1974.

Toulmin, S. *Foresight and Understanding*. Great Britain: Anchor Press, 1961.

West, L. H. T., and A. L. Pines. *Cognitive Structure and Conceptual Change*. Orlando: Academic Press, 1985.

Donna Alvermann

Strategic Teaching in Social Studies

art I of this book presents a framework of instruction that takes into account the research and theory underlying strategic learning and teaching. Part II describes that framework as it is applied in different content areas. This chapter, aimed specifically at promoting strategic teaching in social studies, addresses the following issues:

1. the goals and practices of social studies education in relation to current instructional practices;

2. an application of strategic teaching to social studies; and

3. the implications from the research on proficient and non-proficient learners for strategic teaching.

Goals and Practices in Social Studies Education

According to a recent and fairly comprehensive review of the literature on social studies teaching (Armento 1985), opinions vary widely on what should constitute the goals of social studies education. Traditionally, these goals have been reflected in one of the three most favored ways of teaching social studies: as the transmission of values associated with citizenship, as the structures of the social science disciplines themselves, or as reflective inquiry. More recently, however, evidence from a large-scale survey of a nationally representative sample of high school social studies teachers revealed that literacy skills (i.e., skills largely cognitive in nature) ranked first in a field of eight goals (Rutter 1986). Citizenship ranked a poor fifth.

The lack of consensus on what constitutes an appropriate set of goals for teaching social studies may stem partially from the absence of a comprehensive theory around which consensus could build. Without a theory to guide the design of research investigations or to help in the interpretation of the results of those investigations, there has been little useful knowledge generated for social studies teaching, according to Armento (1985). Armento has also noted that "social studies classrooms of today are little different from those of 20 years ago, despite the expenditure of millions of dollars and the involvement of many creative minds in the development of innovative curricular materials" (p. 944).

All is not as hopeless as it might seem, however. Stake and Easley (1978) found that teachers are generally receptive to learning alternative instructional strategies and to seeking assistance with problems that beset their classrooms. In addition, despite the limitations imposed by an atheoretical framework in which to carry out their investigations, researchers in the area of social studies education are examining many of the same issues that characterize the research of the cognitive scientists. On at least three counts, the models of learning associated with strategic teaching and cognitive instruction are reflected in the current research in social studies teaching.

• *A Common Focus on Higher-Order Thinking.* Currently, both cognitive instruction and social studies research focus on higher-order thinking in the classroom. Articles written for social studies teachers are filled with suggestions on how they might promote reasoning skills (cf. Smith 1985), teach critical thinking using a direct approach (cf. Beyer 1985), or help students ask their own questions (cf. Hunkins 1985). Social studies research, too, is becoming noticeably more focused on the study of thinking in the classroom. For example, a number of researchers have studied the effect of social studies teachers' use of higher cognitive level questions on concept acquisition (cf. Gilmore and McKinney 1986). Although the research findings are mixed, the majority of the evidence indicates that except for elementary students of low socioeconomic status, asking higher cognitive level questions is related to effective teaching (Wilen and Clegg 1986).

Outcomes other than increased student achievement have been reported in studies that varied the cognitive level of questioning. For example, in an observational study of three social studies classes, asking higher level questions that required students to interpret and evaluate information resulted in greater student involvement in classroom activities (Ciardiello 1986).

• *Agreement on the Importance of Background Knowledge.* Models of cognition and cognitive instruction stress the importance of linking new, to-be-learned information to students' prior knowledge and background experience.

93

According to Newmann (1986), for example, one way to engage students' attention and involve them in social studies learning is to schedule activities that are known to link new information with old. He suggests, for example, drawing upon students' prior knowledge through such activities as mock trials, simulations, and oral histories.

A small but growing body of research also supports the practice of tapping students' prior knowledge through prediction activities. Bean and his colleagues (1986), for instance, designed a study in which they taught students how to make predictions about events in history by using a graphic organizer plus options guide. An options guide is a type of study guide that involves students in predicting what course of action (or option) they think a particular historical figure will take. After choosing the option that seems most reasonable to them, students defend their choice of options in small-group discussions. The options guide fosters students' interest in reading the text to see what option the historical figure actually chose. Findings from the Bean et al. study revealed that the organizer plus options guide improved students' performance on a test of near transfer in which students were able to predict without the help of a formal guide.

• *A Common Interest in Promoting Strategic Teaching and Learning.* Currently, the focus for research on social studies teaching and learning is shifting from behavioral questions such as "How do teachers and instruction directly influence learning?" to more cognitively based questions such as "How can teachers influence students to construct . . . meanings of the social world?" (Armento 1985, p. 946). With this shift in focus has come the realization that a repertoire of textbook learning strategies is necessary for students to succeed in constructing meaning from written social studies material. The literature on cognitive instruction is rich in examples of studies that have consistently demonstrated the value of helping students become independent learners through showing them how to use their prior knowledge and the structure of text to make sense of the world in which they live.

In addition to the research on learning from text, smaller segments of social studies research focus on students' use of discussion as a small-group interaction strategy (cf. Tama 1986) and on students' ability to use informal argument analysis (cf. Bruneau 1986). In a related vein, VanSickle's (1985) theoretical analysis of John Dewey's book, *How We Think*, discusses implications for preparing students to engage in reflective thinking strategies such as problem solving, inquiry, hypothesis testing, discovery, and decision making.

Application of Strategic Teaching to Social Studies

Those who wish to incorporate into their repertoire of teaching skills specific insights gained from the research on cognition and cognitive instruction

94

will find in Social Studies Guides 1 and 2, at the end of this chapter, references to the basic reading/thinking processes and text organizational patterns discussed in Part 1 of this book. Social Studies Guide 1 is taken directly from the generic Planning Guide 1 in Part I of this book. Social Studies Guide 2 was rewritten to apply more directly to social studies. The two planning guides can be thought of as menus from which to select a la carte items for inclusion in a lesson of one's own making.

For example, in developing the two-day lesson outlined in Social Studies Guide 3, I used Social Studies Guides 1 and 2 to select appropriate teaching/learning activities for a five-page chapter section on the Progressive Movement. Although in reality I planned only to teach the boxed-in activities in the Social Studies Guide 3, I included other activities as possible alternatives.

The procedure I used to select the three boxed-in activities of Social Studies Guide 3 was simple but systematic. First, I skimmed Social Studies Guides 1 and 2 to familiarize myself with the various categories listed in each guide. Next, I read the to-be-assigned chapter section from the history textbook and made pencil checkmarks in the text margins when I came to information that I wanted students to know. After marking the text in this fashion, I returned to the checked portions of the text to determine which of the reading/thinking processes and text organizational patterns I would select from Social Studies Guides 1 and 2. Finally, I completed the right hand column of Social Studies Guide 3 (the left hand column is merely a repeat of Social Studies Guide 1).

Below is a detailed look at each of the three boxed-in teaching/learning activities mentioned above. They are categorized into one of three lesson parts: preparing for learning, presenting the content, and applying/integrating. It should be noted that some activities extend over more than one lesson part. That is both natural and desirable. Each lesson part also contains two alternatives to the boxed-in activity.

Preparing for Learning

The Vocabulary Overview Guide (Carr 1985) is an activity for improving students' ability to acquire meanings for words that they will be exposed to in their content area texts (see Figure 5.1). If presented systematically (i.e., teacher demonstration and explanation followed by guided student practice and independent practice), students should be able to adapt and apply the Vocabulary Overview Guide in their various subject matter classes.

The Vocabulary Overview Guide incorporates several of the insights gained from cognitive research on prior knowledge. For instance, in the guide in Figure 5.2, which I developed for a unit on the Progressive Movement, students had to use their prior knowledge of the word "start" as a clue to remem-

Figure 5.1. The Vocabulary Overview Guide

Define the vocabulary through the use of context.

1. Survey the material (title, heading) to see what it is about.
2. Skim the material to identify unknown vocabulary words and underline them.
3. Try to figure out the meaning of the word from the context of the sentences around it. Ask someone or use a dictionary to check the meaning.
4. Write the definitions in the text (use pencil) or on paper so that they will be available when you read the text.

Read the passage.

5. Read the passage with the defined vocabulary to ensure comprehension.

Complete the Vocabulary Overview Guide.

6. Fill in your Vocabulary Overview Guide. Write:
    a. the *title* of the passage
    b. the *category titles* (Decide on the categories you need by asking yourself the topics the vocabulary described or discussed.)
    c. the *vocabulary word*
    d. the *definition* underneath the vocabulary word (You can use synonyms here. Make sure you leave room to add a few more synonyms as your vocabulary increases.)
    e. a *clue* to help you connect the meaning to something you know or have experienced.

Study the vocabulary.

7. Read the title and categories to activate background knowledge and recall words associated with each aspect of the story.
8. When you study the word in each category, cover the clue and word meaning. Uncover the clue if necessary. If the clue doesn't jog your memory, then uncover the meaning.
9. Review your words frequently (each day) until you know them well. Review them once a week or periodically as you learn more words.
10. Add synonyms to old vocabulary words as you learn them. In this way you will connect the old with the new words, and that will help you remember them.

Reprinted from *Teaching Reading As Thinking*

bering the meaning of a targeted (or new) word ("initiative"). They also had to apply their prior knowledge of what it means "to start something" in order to arrive at a definition for the targeted word—"to introduce or start legislation."

An alternative to using the Vocabulary Overview Guide is a strategy developed by Kuse and Kuse (1986) called Using Analogies to Preview Text. This strategy is particularly useful when the content contains many difficult concepts, with which most students have had no previous experience. This strategy can be effective in building students' awareness of the need to adjust their rate and approach to reading. Briefly, Using Analogies to Preview Text involves students in describing how they feel when they read a difficult passage. If a simile were used, as in the example below, students would be encouraged first to preview the text and then to complete the following sentence: "Reading densely packed material with lots of new facts is like ＿＿＿＿＿＿＿＿＿＿." By examining students' completed sentences, teachers gain an understanding of how difficult the text is for certain individuals. This knowledge of difficulty level can then be used in planning for future lessons.

Another preparatory activity is the Prediction Guide (Herber 1978). It is

Figure 5.2. Vocabulary Overview Guide

CHAPTER TITLE *The Progressive Movement*

(category title)	(category title)
Aims	*Reforms*

(target word) / (target word)

★ *restore* ★ *initiative*

(clues) / (clues)

old *start*

(definitions) / (definitions)

put back as it was *introduce legislation*

★ *industrialism* ★ *primary*

factory *early*

manufacturing *a "nominating" election*

★ *economic* ★ *suffrage*

money *E.R.A.*

human needs, comforts *right to vote*

appropriate for focusing students' interests or in setting purposes for reading a particular section of a text. The Prediction Guide makes use of students' prior knowledge about a topic by asking them to respond to a series of topic-related statements. The statements call for responses based on what students think they know as well as on whether they think the author of their textbook will agree with their responses. After reading the text, the students are encouraged to discuss why they marked a statement the way they did.

Presenting the Content

The Structural Organizer Plus Grid (Slater, Graves, and Piche 1985) benefits students as they read because it makes them aware of the text's overall pattern of organization. Knowledge of how the text is organized has been shown repeatedly to be of value in helping students comprehend and retain what they read. In a study of ninth graders' ability to comprehend and recall information from a history textbook, Slater and his colleagues found that students who filled in an outline grid while they read a text passage accompanied by a structural organizer were helped significantly to remember what they had read. The Structural Organizer Plus Grid gave students advance notice about the author's plan for organizing the material; it also made clear to students how they could use that organizational plan as they read their assignment.

The Structural Organizer Plus Grid that I developed, with the help of a group of tenth-grade students, was intended for use with the Progressive Movement portion of text discussed earlier. To enable students to examine their texts for the purpose of determining the author's organizational plan, I involved them in a ten-minute discussion that focused on the following points:

- the importance of recognizing how a text is organized;
- the clues that tell us the Progressive Movement text is organized around a problem and its several solutions;
- the understanding that the problem/solution organizational pattern is frequently an author's choice for organizing social studies text.

Following the discussion, students read a portion of the text on the Progressive Movement and completed the grid below (see Figure 5.3). After several lessons in which students were provided guidance in determining text structure and in evaluating the usefulness of the grid, they were ready to experiment with constructing their own grids, based on their own analyses of the text.

The Structural Organizer Plus Grid is a useful activity when the goal of instruction is to help students construct meaning for a given text segment by making use of the author's organizational plan. However, it does not assist students in confirming any predictions they may have made prior to reading the selec-

Figure 5.3. Grid for The Progressive Movement

Problem: _Demand that privileges handed out by the government be controlled_

Example 1 _Restore control of government to common people_

Example 2 _Correct the abuses and injustices brought on by industrialism_

Example 3 _Restore equality of economic opportunity_

Actions taken by:

Group 1 _Leaders like "Fighting Bob" La Follette_

Group 2 _Women reformers_

Group 3 _Muckrakers_

Solutions:

1 _Australian ballot_

2 _Initiative, referendum, recall_

3 _Direct Primary_

4 _Women's suffrage_

5 _Direct election of Senators_

6 _Reform of city government_

tion. To assist students in the latter task, Herber's (1978) Prediction Guide is recommended. Using the Prediction Guide, students have the opportunity first to predict whether or not an author will agree or disagree with the predictions they have made about a particular portion of text. After reading the text, they must cite evidence from it that supports (or fails to support) their predictions. Because the Prediction Guide is designed to foster small group discussions, students have an opportunity to demonstrate their oral reasoning abilities as they engage in higher order reading and thinking skills.

Clarifying ideas during reading is an extremely important activity and one

99

that is addressed in the content reading heuristic known as Listen-Read-Discuss, or L-R-D for short (Manzo and Casale 1985, p. 733). The L-R-D provides teachers with an instructional activity that makes use of students' prior knowledge, optimizes the effectiveness of minilectures, and approximates the steps of a Directed Reading Activity. Briefly, the steps of the L-R-D are these:

1. Choose a particularly well-organized and well-written portion of the text to introduce this activity.

2. Provide students with a minilecture about that portion of the text.

3. Direct students to read the pages in the text that cover the material they just listened to in the minilecture.

4. Involve students in a post-reading discussion of the assigned text in which basic understandings are clarified and critical questions are raised. The following questions are suggested as a means of evoking the type of discussion specified above:

- What did you understand best from what you read?
- What did you understand least well from what you heard and read?
- What questions or thoughts did this lesson raise in your mind?

Applying and Integrating

Frequently, social studies teachers ask students to explain in writing "why" some event occurred as part of a post-reading assignment. Although teachers may have the expository essay in mind as an appropriate vehicle for the students' thoughts, the students are likely to fall into what Duthie (1986, p. 232) calls the "narrative trap." That is, they are likely to write about *what* happened without attempting to analyze *why* it happened. To counteract students' tendency to write in the narrative form when the expository essay is the expected product, Duthie developed a web outline that provides a logical structure for the essay. The web consists of a question, a "yes" and a "no" strand so that one can discuss both sides of the question, a thesis, and a conclusion. It is drawn as shown in Figure 5.4.

Having outlined the basic logical structure of an argument, students are now ready to think of supporting data from their textbooks or other sources that can be appended to the "yes" and "no" strands. The thesis and conclusion are written last. Besides providing a structure for the analytical essay, the web highlights imbalances in one's argument or points up places where one's argument is not supported by any data. Also, the teacher can use the web as an objective marking key for the completed essay. When the marked web is returned along with the expository essay, the student has a graphic idea of where the strengths and weaknesses are in his or her writing.

Adaptive Webbing (Alvermann 1986) is an extension of Duthie's web outline. It differs in three ways:

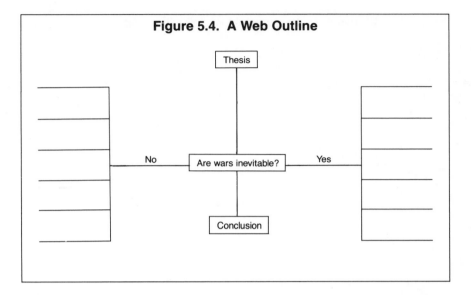

Figure 5.4. A Web Outline

1. Adaptive Webbing takes into account differences in students' ability level and enables both low- and high-achieving students to work at a level of difficulty that is appropriate for them.

2. Adaptive Webbing signals the differences in difficulty level of the task (Bloom et al. 1956) by its use of coded geometrical shapes. For example, rectangles signify writing tasks that require students to simply recall information; triangles signify writing tasks that require students to compare and contrast arguments; and ovals signify writing tasks that require students to generate criteria for evaluating whether an action was justified.

3. Adaptive Webbing provides structure for whole-class discussions about an assigned segment of text. It encourages both low- and high-achieving students to engage in higher-order thinking.

Figure 5.5 is an example of how Adaptive Webbing was applied to the chapter section on the Progressive Movement. Note that although the logical structures for all three levels of writing difficulty were included, students who were assigned to write a basic analytic essay were signalled to attend only to the information within the rectangles. Students who needed the challenge of comparing and contrasting two arguments were signaled to attend to the information within the triangles, and so on.

Sometimes social studies teachers prefer to choose an applying/integrating activity that helps them assess whether students have achieved the purpose(s) of the lesson. When one of those purposes involves generating new

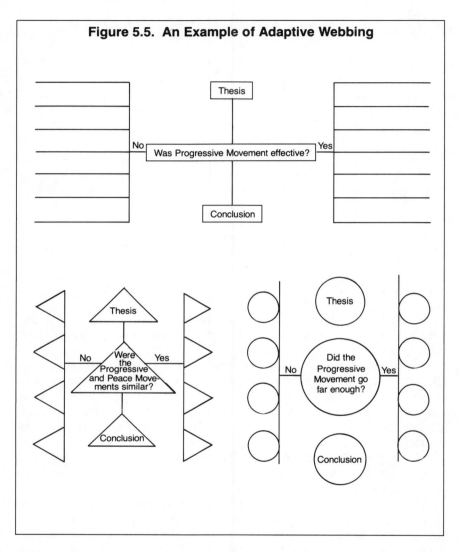

Figure 5.5. An Example of Adaptive Webbing

questions about the topic under study, an activity known as Group Reading for Different Purposes (Dolan et al. 1979) is appropriate. The GRDP involves students in small group work while they are generating the questions. Then, the questions are shared in a general class discussion. Some suggestions for the types of prompts that can be placed on 3″ × 5″ cards and then passed out to the small groups for their input follow.

1. Make up three questions that state a fact about the material you have just read. Then make up three questions that offer an opinion about the material. Ask the class to determine which is which.

2. Devise a set of questions that can be answered only by consulting a reference source other than your textbook.

3. Present an alternative argument to support an explanation given in your text. Then ask the class to determine which argument is the stronger—the textbook's or the group's.

Another applying/integrating activity that social studies teachers who are interested in transfer of learning might consider is the Co-operative Lesson on Conflict Resolution (Morton 1986). Because this activity involves students in conflict, it is important that they have had some previous practice in criticizing ideas and not people, listening to others, and taking different perspectives. The lesson requires two or three one-hour periods to complete. On the first day, students are divided randomly into groups of four and then paired within those groups so that one pair becomes the proponents of an idea and the other pair becomes the opponents. Even though the pairs oppose each other, eventually they will write *one* report at the end of the activity. Next, the teacher explains the scenario. For example, it is the day after the United States has attacked Libya for its role in international terrorism. The CIA reports retaliatory plans by the Syrians. Do you go ahead with a raid on Damascus? You will have to make a written report to President Reagan at the end of the activity. The students have approximately 20 to 30 minutes to prepare their arguments. On the second day, the pairs debate the issue within the following time structure:

5 minutes—about a minute for each student to present his or her stance on the issue,

10 minutes—open discussion,

10 minutes—reverse perspectives/roles,

10 minutes—consensus is reached by group of four, and

15 minutes—report written by whole group.

The final step in this activity is an evaluation of the group process. For instance, what went well in your group? What would you do differently next time?

Implications from Research on Proficient and Less Proficient Learners

For cognitive instruction in the social studies classroom to be beneficial to all students, regardless of achievement level, teachers must be aware of at least two insights from the current thinking and research on proficient and less proficient learners. First, teachers must be cognizant of the relationship between the goals of social studies education and their own expectations of students.

Second, social studies teachers must be alert to the research findings that differentiate the proficient learner from the less proficient learner if they are to be effective in their instructional interventions. In short, this awareness on the part of teachers is essential if Social Studies Guides 1, 2, and 3, at the end of this chapter, are to be put to their proper use.

Knowledge of Goals and Expectations

According to Cherryholmes (1985), "... the goal of social studies is to transmit knowledge about society along with such skills as analysis, decision making, and critical thinking to students" (p. 395). Although Engle (1986) challenges the idea of transmitting knowledge, preferring instead to "... offer up opportunities for children to question" (p. 22), nonetheless he agrees with Cherryholmes that *all* students need to be taught how to participate in social studies learning. That is, regardless of ability or achievement level, students must be shown how to collect evidence, link that evidence to a conclusion, and then justify the conclusion. Concerning participation, Cherryholmes adds, "Not all students can participate at the same level of competence, but they can all participate" (1985, p. 399).

As an example of how teachers might enable all students to participate in a history lesson, Moore, Alouf, and Needham (1984) offer these three suggestions: (1) Use advance (or graphic) organizers to help students understand the hierarchical arrangement of historical concepts; (2) move from the concrete to the abstract; and (3) teach the core concepts of history so that students have a "road map" of the discipline.

Differences in Proficiency Levels

Researchers have studied a number of strategic learning behaviors that differentiate the proficient from less proficient learner. Findings from several of these research studies follow.

1. Generally, proficient learners understand the demands of different tasks and are able to discriminate among those demands in selecting an approach to complete a specific task. For instance, they are able to judge whether their knowledge level will permit them to complete a reading task successfully (Baker and Brown 1984). To help the less proficient learners in their classrooms, it may be useful for teachers to select activities from Social Studies Guide 3 that structure tasks for students.

2. Proficient learners are able to adjust their reading behaviors to suit their purpose for reading (e.g., reading rapidly for the gist of a selection vs. reading more slowly to remember the details). Less proficient learners, on the other hand, do not exhibit this flexibility in purposeful reading; they use the

same behaviors for both (Baker and Brown 1984). Teachers can assist these less proficient learners by instructing them in how to use an author's organizational plan as a help in deciding what to spend time on and what to skim over in the text they've been assigned to read.

3. Learners of any age and ability level are more likely to take responsibility for applying whatever skills they have acquired when they are faced with tasks that are neither too difficult nor too easy (Wagoner 1983). It is useful, therefore, to take into account individual differences when planning for instruction.

4. Proficient learners engage in fix-up strategies on their own when they recognize they have failed to comprehend the text. Less proficient readers, on the other hand, are not aware that they can exercise control over their failure to comprehend (DiVesta, Hayward, and Orlando 1979). The implication for teachers is to know which activities to select from Social Studies Guide 3. An activity that shows students how to accommodate old information in light of new information may be preferable, for instance, to one that asks questions.

These findings suggest that strategic teaching will have to be adapted for proficient and less proficient learners. What those adaptations will look like will depend to a great extent upon individual teachers' interpretations of the information presented in Social Studies Guides 1 and 2, and most certainly upon the choices they make in planning their own instructional guides.

Summary

This chapter has addressed three issues. First, it has attempted to relate the goals of social studies education to current instructional practices. Second, it has demonstrated how the insights gained from research on cognition and cognitive instruction and the concept of strategic teaching can be applied to social studies teaching. Specifically, Social Studies Guides 1, 2, and 3 have been presented for the purpose of helping teachers select appropriate activities for preparing, presenting, and applying/integrating. Third, the chapter has presented implications from research on proficient and less proficient learners for social studies teaching.

Social Studies Guide 1

Thinking Processes	*Instructional Strategies*

PREPARING FOR LEARNING   **PREPARING FOR LEARNING**

Comprehend objective/task
define learning objectives
consider task/audience
determine criteria for success

Preview/Select materials/cues at hand
skim features and graphic aids
determine content focus/organizational pattern

Activate prior knowledge
access content and vocabulary
access categories and structure
access strategies/plans

Focus interest/Set purpose
form hypotheses and questions/make predictions
represent/organize ideas (categorize/outline)

ON-LINE PROCESSING (Text Segments)   **PRESENTING THE CONTENT**

Modify Hypotheses/Clarify ideas

check hypotheses, predictions, questions
compare to prior knowledge
ask clarification questions
examine logic of argument, flow of ideas
generate new questions

Integrate ideas
select important concepts/words
connect and organize ideas, summarize

Assimilate new ideas
articulate changes in knowledge
evaluate ideas/products
withhold judgment

CONSOLIDATING/EXTENDING ("The Big Picture")   **APPLYING/INTEGRATING**

Integrate/organize meaning for whole
categorize and integrate information, conclude
summarize key ideas and connections
evaluate/revise/edit

Assess achievement of purpose/learning
compare new learnings to prior knowledge
identify gaps in learning and information
generate new questions/next steps

Extend learning
translate/apply to new situations
rehearse and study

Social Studies Guide 2
Patterns of Organization and Analysis in Social Studies

1. *Goal Frame.* This frame consists of the Goal (something that is desired by an individual or a group), the Action taken to attain that Goal, and the Outcome or consequence of the Action. The Outcome may either satisfy or fail to satisfy the individual(s) seeking the Goal. Many historical texts fit the Goal frame, according to Armbruster and Anderson (1985). Among the examples they give is Hitler's goal of preserving the "master race" which resulted in the murder of six million Jews.

2. *Problem/Solution Frame.* This frame is a variation on the Goal Frame. In the Problem/Solution frame, the Problem can be "an event, a condition, or series of events or conditions resulting in a state that is an obstacle to the attainment of the Goal" (Armbruster and Anderson 1985, p. 95). When the Problem is tackled, however, a Solution follows. This sequence of events is equivalent to the Action and Outcome of the Goal Frame. Armbruster and Anderson list voyages of discovery as social studies content that fits into the Problem/Solution frame. For example, when the Europeans wanted to trade with the Far East, they encountered several problems, such as dangerous journeys and the high prices of Italian goods.

3. *Cultures Frame.* The major categories of information necessary for defining the Cultures frame include: Technology (food, clothing, shelter, tools); Institutions (economic, political, family, religious, educational); Language; and the Arts. Comparisons and contrasts of these categories make it possible to differentiate one culture from another (Armbruster and Anderson 1985). For instance, the cultures of Islamic countries can be differentiated on the basis of food preferences, political parties, language, and music.

4. *People Frame.* Authors of social studies textbooks use this frame to present biographical information about individuals who are mentioned in the main body of the text. Frequently, this information appears in highlighted or boxed off areas in the margins of the text. The People frame contains these categories: Background (period of time they lived and the significant events in their lives); Traits (personality, habits); Goals (personal beliefs that motivated them to act in a particular way); and Accomplishments (significant contributions that they made). Armbruster and Anderson (1985) provide as an example of the People frame, Frederick Douglass, who was born a slave and who learned to read under unusual circumstances (Background). The People frame that included information on Douglass might describe his personal desire to be free and to abolish slavery as an institution of American life (Goals). This frame might also point out Douglass' talents as speaker, a leader, and a newspaper editor (Traits), which made him famous as one of the black abolitionists (Accomplishment).

5. *Descriptive Frames.* Descriptive frames and categories depend somewhat on the nature of what is being described. In geography, for example, *regions* are always described within the following five superordinate categories: land (physical features, climate, and natural resources); people (social/cultural, education, religion); cities; economy; and government (Armbruster and Anderson 1985, Herber 1978).

6. *Compare/Contrast Two or More Things.* Like description, the categories for comparison and contrast differ according to what is being compared or contrasted. However, *comparisons* should always establish clearly how the things (people, places, events, ideas, etc.) are similar, giving examples or further description to support the generalization. Similarly, *contrast analyses* must state explicitly all the ways in which the things are different as well as illustrate each difference (Jones, Amiran, and Katims 1985).

7. *Interaction Frames: Conflict/Cooperation.* Much of history involves the interaction of two or more persons or groups. To comprehend the nature of their interaction, the key questions are: What are the persons/groups? What were their goals? What was the nature of their interaction: conflict or cooperation? How did they act and react? What was the outcome for each person/group? (Jones 1985).

8. *Interaction Frames: Causal Interaction.* To understand the causal interaction of a *complex event* such as an election or a *complex phenomenon* such as the causes of juvenile delinquency, the critical task involves answering the following questions: What are the factors that cause X? Which ones are most important? How do the factors interrelate? Do some factors occur before others? Are the factors that cause X initially the same as those that account for its persistence?

Social Studies Guide 3

Thinking Processes	*Instructional Strategies*
PREPARING FOR LEARNING	**PREPARING FOR LEARNING**
Comprehend objective/task define learning objectives consider task/audience determine criteria for success	
Preview/Select materials/cues at hand skim features and graphic aids determine content focus/organizational pattern	Using Analogies to Preview Text (Kuse and Kuse 1986)
Activate prior knowledge access content and vocabulary access categories and structure access strategies/plans	Vocabulary Overview Guide (Carr 1985)
Focus interest/Set purpose form hypotheses and questions/make predictions represent/organize ideas (categorize/outline)	Prediction Guide (Part 1) (Herber 1978)
ON-LINE PROCESSING (Text Segments)	**PRESENTING THE CONTENT**
Modify Hypotheses/Clarify ideas check hypotheses, predictions,questions compare to prior knowledge ask clarification questions examine logic of argument, flow of ideas generate new questions	Listen-Read-Discuss: A Content Reading Heuristic (Manzo and Casale 1985)
Integrate ideas select important concepts/words connect and organize ideas, summarize	Structural Organizer Plus Grid (Slater, Graves, and Piche)
Assimilate new ideas articulate changes in knowledge evaluate ideas/products withhold judgment	Prediction Guide (Part 2) (Herber 1978)
CONSOLIDATING/EXTENDING (''The Big Picture'')	**APPLYING AND INTEGRATING**
Integrate/organize meaning for whole categorize and integrate information, conclude summarize key ideas and connections evaluate/revise/edit	Adaptive Webbing (Alvermann 1986)
Assess achievement of purpose/learning compare new learnings to prior knowledge identify gaps in learning and information generate new questions/next steps	Group Reading for Different Purposes (Dolan et al. 1979)
Extend learning translate/apply to new situations rehearse and study	Co-operative Lesson on Conflict Resolution (Morton 1986)

References

Alvermann, D. E. "Adaptive Webbing." Paper presented at the Baltimore City School Staff Development Day, Baltimore, August 1986.

Armbruster, B. B., and T. H. Anderson. "Frames: Structure for Informational Texts." In *Technology of Text*, Vol. 2, edited by D. H. Jonassen. Englewood Cliffs, N.J.: Educational Technology Publications, 1985.

Armento, B. J. "Research on Teaching Social Studies." In *Handbook of Research on Teaching*, 3rd ed., edited by M. C. Wittrock. New York: Macmillan, 1985.

Baker, L., and A. L. Brown. "Cognitive Monitoring in Reading." In *Understanding Reading Comprehension*, edited by J. Flood. Newark, Del.: International Reading Association, 1984.

Bean, T. W., J. Sorter, H. Singer, and C. Frazee. "Teaching Students How to Make Predictions About Events in History with a Graphic Organizer Plus Options Guide." *Journal of Reading* 29 (1986): 739-745.

Beyer, B. K. "Teaching Critical Thinking: A Direct Approach." *Social Education* 49 (1985): 297-303.

Bloom, B. S., M. Engelhart, E. Furst, W. Hill, and D. Krathwohl, eds. *Taxonomy of Educational Objectives: Handbook 1. Cognitive Domain*. New York: David McKay, 1956.

Bruneau, W. "The Pleasures and Perils of Inference." *The History and Social Science Teacher* 21 (1986): 165-175.

Carr, E. "The Vocabulary Overview Guide: A Metacognitive Strategy to Improve Vocabulary Comprehension and Retention." *Journal of Reading* 21 (1985): 684-689.

Cherryholmes, C. H. "Language and Discourse in Social Studies Education." *Social Education* 49 (1985): 395-399.

Ciardiello, A. V. "Teacher Questioning and Student Interaction: An Observation of Three Social Studies Classes." *The Social Studies* 77 (1986): 119-122.

DiVesta, F. J., K. G. Hayward, and V. P. Orlando. "Developmental Trends in Monitoring Text for Comprehension." *Child Development* 50 (1979): 97-105.

Dolan, T., E. Dolan, V. Taylor, J. Shoreland, and C. Harrison. "Improving Reading Through Group Discussion Activities." In *The Effective Use of Reading*, edited by E. Lunzer and K. Gardner. London: Heinemann Educational Books, 1979.

Duthie, J. "The Web: A Powerful Tool for the Teaching and Evaluation of the Expository Essay." *The History and Social Science Teacher* 21 (1986): 232-236.

Engle, S. H. "Late Night Thoughts About the New Social Studies." *Social Education* 50 (1986): 20-22.

Gilmore, A. C., and C. W. McKinney. "The Effects of Student Questions and Teacher Questions on Concept Acquisition." *Theory and Research in Social Education* 14 (1986): 225-244.

Herber, H. L. *Teaching Reading in Content Areas*. 2nd ed. Englewood Cliffs, N.J.: Prentice-Hall, 1978.

Hunkins, F. P. "Helping Students Ask Their Own Questions." *Social Education* 49 (1985): 293-296.

Jones, B. F. "Research-based Guidelines for Constructing Graphic Representations of Text." Paper presented at the annual meeting of the American Educational Research Association, Chicago, April 1985.

Jones, B. F., M. R. Amiran, and M. Katims. "Teaching Cognitive Strategies and Text Structures Within Language Arts Programs." In *Thinking and Learning Skills: Relating*

Instruction to Research, Vol. 1, edited by J. Segal, S. F. Chipman, and R. Glaser. Hillsdale, N.J.: Erlbaum, 1985.

Kuse, L. S., and H. R. Kuse. "Using Analogies to Study Social Studies Text." *Social Education* 50 (1986): 24-25.

Manzo, A. V., and U. P. Casale. "Listen-Read-Discuss: A Content Reading Heuristic." *Journal of Reading* 28 (1985): 732-734.

Moore, J., J. L. Alouf, and J. Needham. "Cognitive Development and Historical Reasoning in Social Studies Curriculum." *Theory and Research in Social Education* 12 (1984): 49-64.

Morton, T. "Decision on Dieppe: A Co-operative Lesson on Conflict Resolution." *The History and Social Science Teacher* 21 (1986): 237-241.

Newmann, F. M. "Priorities for the Future: Toward a Common Agenda." *Social Education* 50 (1986): 240-250.

Rutter, R. A. "Profile of the Profession." *Social Education* 50 (1986): 252-255.

Slater, W., M. F. Graves, and G. L. Piche. "Effects of Structural Organizers on Ninth Grade Students' Comprehension and Recall of Four Patterns of Expository Text." *Reading Research Quarterly* 20 (1985): 189-202.

Smith, A. "Promoting Reasoning Skills: An Interdisciplinary Approach." *The Social Studies* 76 (1985): 260-263.

Stake, R. E., and J. A. Easley. *Case Studies in Science Education*. Washington, D.C.: National Science Foundation, 1978.

Tama, M. C. "How Are Students Responding in Discussion Groups?" *The Social Studies* 77 (1986): 132-135.

VanSickle, R. L. "Research Implications of a Theoretical Analysis of John Dewey's *How We Think*." *Theory and Research in Social Education* 13 (1985): 1-20.

Wagoner, S. A. "Comprehension Monitoring: What It Is and What We Know About It." *Reading Research Quarterly* 18 (1983): 328-346.

Wilen, W. W., and A. A. Clegg, Jr. "Effective Questions and Questioning: A Research Review." *Theory and Research in Social Education* 14 (1986): 153-161.

Mary Montgomery Lindquist

6

Strategic Teaching in Mathematics

"**M**athematics" is the common answer to the question: What subject in high school requires the most thinking? Yet many of us in mathematics education deplore the lack of thinking in mathematics. Davis (1984, p. 349) describes a series of "disaster studies" that "show in detail how many students, believed to be successful when one judges them by typical tests, are revealed as seriously confused when one looks more closely at how they think about the subject." Comparison of the results of the national mathematics assessments conducted by the National Assessment of Educational Progress (NAEP) shows a great disparity between performance on routine exercises and items that required thinking. While the overall performance of younger students (ages 9 and 13) improved from the second to the third assessment, the increase could be accounted for by routine exercises. Analysis of individual items showed that performance had decreased on those requiring thinking or understanding (NAEP 1983).

The purpose of this chapter is not to solve the dilemma of whether we do or do not teach thinking in mathematics. Actually, this is probably not an either/ or situation, but one that depends on how you regard thinking (e.g., Skemp 1978). In particular, the purpose is to consider the application of research on cognition, cognitive instruction, and strategic teaching to mathematics instruction. The chapter is organized to address three questions: (1) To what extent does the framework for learning and instruction presented in Part I of this book apply to mathematics? (2) Can the generic planning guides in Part I be used to plan sequences of instruction in mathematics? and (3) What adaptations, if any, are needed to teach less proficient students?

Parallels of Learning/Teaching Assumptions in Mathematics

"Parallels, angles, and skewed lines" may have been a more appropriate title for this section. At times, the ideas proposed in Chapters 1 and 2 are quite parallel to those in mathematics. For other concepts, the proposed ideas and mathematics begin at the same point but move in different directions, thus creating angles. And finally, at times the two areas are like skewed lines in different planes. In particular, those ideas related to learning seem to be quite consistent; those related to teaching seem to have a common base; and those related to organizational patterns seem to be askew.

Learning

There has been substantial progress in recent years in the understanding of children's cognitions, especially in certain mathematical domains (e.g., Resnick and Ford 1981, Lesh and Landau 1983, Davis 1984, Romberg and Carpenter 1986). This research along with the research on problem solving (e.g., Silver 1985, Schoenfeld 1985a) provides a wealth of information about thinking in mathematics. Although certainly not conclusive or exhaustive, it does provide a basis for examining the parallels between language arts and mathematics. There appear to be six themes in the discussion in Chapter 1 that are also central to mathematics.

1. Just as there is a need for a new definition of reading, there is a need for cognitively based mathematics programs. Practitioners such as Burns (1985, p. 14) have summarized the state of elementary mathematics as follows:

In traditional instruction, the primary goal is to develop computational competence. The emphasis is often on getting right answers, enough right answers to earn good grades or to do well on standardized tests. The teacher or the answer key is the source for revealing to the students the correctness of their answers. And, sadly, it's the quick right answer that is often valued more than the thinking that leads to that answer. What is missing is attention to children's deciding on the reasonableness of their solutions, justifying their procedures, verbalizing their processes, reflecting on their thinking—all those behaviors that contribute to the development of mathematical thinking.

The National Council of Teachers of Mathematics (NCTM 1980) proposed in the *Agenda for Action* that problem solving be the focus of mathematics instruction. This recommendation has influenced the current curricular mate-rials; hopefully, it will also affect students' learning. While this is a laudable goal, it is often interpreted as treating problem solving as a topic. Many (e.g., Lindquist 1984, Kilpatrick 1981) have cautioned that the focus should be inter-preted as taking a problem-solving approach, or a thinking approach, to the learning of mathematics, not as treating problem solving as a separate topic.

Similarly, researchers have called for a cognitively based approach. For ex-ample, Fennema, Carpenter, and Peterson (1986) are presently studying what they have termed "cognitively guided instruction." Resnick and Ford (1981, p. 246) write about emerging themes in the psychology of mathematics that "give a sense of the possibilities and directions for a new, cognitively grounded in-structional psychology."

It is important to note that this need is felt not by one group alone, but by teachers, curriculum developers, and researchers in mathematics education. Thus, it is timely to consider thinking in mathematics and its relationship to other curricular areas.

2. Constructing meaning is at the heart of a mathematics curriculum based on cognitive learning, just as it is in other curricular areas. While there is some disagreement about how certain meanings are constructed (see Car-penter's review of Steffe's work, 1985a), and there is still a need for evidence about how new knowledge is integrated into established knowledge structures (Resnick and Ford 1981), a body of research helpful to the practitioner is begin-ning to emerge.

The clearest picture of how children construct meanings comes from the mathematics content area called "early number work." Within this area, the re-search on beginning addition and subtraction has been developed to the point of giving guidance for instruction. (See Carpenter 1985b for a recent summary.) In examining this research, it is evident that young children do construct meaning from problems. For example, at the stage when children are solving problems by directly representing or modeling, they will solve the following two "subtraction problems" according to the semantic structure of the problem.

Problem A: Jill had 8 trucks. She gave 3 to Bill.
            How many trucks does she have left?
Problem B: Jill has 8 trucks. Bill has 6 trucks.
            How many more trucks does Jill have than Bill?

In representing Problem A, a young child counts out 8 trucks and gives 3 away. Then, the child counts how many trucks are left. In Problem B, the child counts out 8 trucks and a set of 6 trucks, matches Jill's trucks with Bill's and counts to see how many more Jill has. Watching young children as they approach these problems, one is convinced that they have constructed meaning. What is discouraging is to watch second graders struggle with the same types of problems when they are relying only on the strategy of answering the question: "Do I add or subtract?" Without helping children build the constructs necessary to answer this question, we encourage them not to think about the semantics of the problem and perhaps encourage them to think about other avenues of solving the problem such as what are the key words, what size numbers are there, how many numbers are there—all thinking strategies that can lead to misconceptions. A more in-depth discussion of this problem is given by Hiebert (1984).

In summary, there is much in the research in mathematics education that encourages taking a constructive point of view and there is guidance to do so in certain mathematical areas.

3. Another similarity with the proposed view of cognition is that learning mathematics is not linear but is highly *recursive*. Kilpatrick's (1986) plenary address to the Fifth International Congress of Mathematical Education was entitled "Reflection and Recursion." He cites an example of learning as recursion from the theory of geometric learning by the van Hieles. They pose that as learners move from level to level of thought in geometry, they return to the same concepts but give new meanings to these concepts (see a more complete description in Fuys, Geddes, and Tischler 1984). Certainly, the previously mentioned research on addition and subtraction is indicative of recursive learning. Children continue to build new meanings for addition and subtraction as they are presented with a variety of additive or subtractive situations. For example, their first meaning of subtraction may be separating, and later they will add the comparative meaning.

Although much has been written about reflective thinking, there is little in the mathematics literature directed toward recursive thinking. Kilpatrick (1986, p. 11) claims that "both reflection and recursion, when applied to cognition, are ways of becoming conscious of, and getting control over, one's concepts and procedures. To turn a concept over in mind and to operate on a procedure with itself can enable the thinker to think how to think, and may help the learner learn how to learn." It seems logical that thinking is recursive; certainly from reflecting on one's own thinking one would conclude that it is nonlinear. Yet the question remains how recursion occurs and how to help learners develop the ability to think recursively.

4. As the model reader, writer, listener, or speaker has a repertoire of cognitive strategies, so does the model mathematics learner. In fact, so does the "nonmodel" mathematics learner, but this repertoire may be filled with misconceptions. First, we will consider a selection of productive strategies, and

114

then we will look at some fraught with misconceptions because they also tell us about thinking.

There are productive strategies in mathematics related to particular content areas and more generic ones often associated with problem solving. A large body of research has been amassed on how children derive basic addition facts. For example, a child may think through the sum of 5 and 6 by relating it to the known fact, 5 + 5, as follows: "I know that 5 and 5 is 10, 5 and 6 is one more, or 11." Or a child may think through 8 + 7 as follows: "9, 10 and 5 more is 15." There is also evidence that instruction which explicitly teaches these strategies is more effective than instruction that relies only on memorization of isolated facts. (Steinberg 1985; Thornton, Jones, and Toohey 1983).

Instruction in problem solving tends to center on general heuristics such as drawing a picture, writing a mathematical sentence, and other translation strategies or on other strategies such as making a table, solving a simpler problem, or working backwards. While this may be one step forward from omitting problem-solving instruction altogether, teaching these strategies is not sufficient. Just as conceptual knowledge and procedural knowledge are necessary prior knowledge in solving problems, these problem-solving heuristics are also. It may be that we have looked at them as the basis for thinking and *the* key to solving problems, when indeed they are just a slightly different type of procedural knowledge than, say, that of the multiplication algorithm. For example, consider the following problem:

Find the area of a rectangular plot whose length is three more feet than its width and whose perimeter is 26 feet.

One must have prior conceptual knowledge about area, length, width, perimeter, and rectangle, and prior procedural knowledge about how to find area and perimeter. Yet, even with this knowledge, many children cannot solve this problem. They may be lacking the knowledge of the heuristic of how to draw a helpful picture and how to approach the problem by guess and check. Even with these added general heuristic strategies in their repertoire, we cannot be assured they will be able to solve the problem. It is the interaction of metacognitive (or conditional thinking) strategies that may be the missing link.

These cognitive strategies just described are productive, but we must also be aware of the strategies that are counterproductive. The literature is filled with mathematical misconceptions of students (see Brown 1978, Resnick and Ford 1981, David 1984, Schoenfeld 1985a, Shaughnessy 1985). One of my most vivid memories of teaching my first college mathematics class is of a student who said, "If I do everything just backwards from the way I think I should, then I know it will be right." How I wished I had pursued her thoughts and yet, even then, I had enough samples of students' work with isolated facts or rote learning that I knew what she meant, or at least how she felt. What is scary is that her strategy worked; she was an "A" student!

The most common subtraction error of nine-year-olds (Carpenter, Corbitt, Kepner, Lindquist, and Reys 1981) is a reversal error. This error produces the following answer:

$$
\begin{array}{r}
394 \\
-\,157 \\
\hline
243
\end{array}
$$

Children who respond this way may well be thinking: "Always subtract the smaller number from the larger." They have not yet built the construct of three digits being one number, or they fail to coordinate this knowledge with the procedure of how to handle the digits in the ones place.

Fischbein and his associates (1985) have shown how primitive models used in initial instructions of multiplication and division may influence misconceptions of the broader meanings and applications of these operations. Their studies show that when we do not help learners build more sophisticated models, other than the formal mathematical model, that students revert to primitive thinking.

What is important about noting errors is the clue to how a learner is thinking. We have often waited until an error has appeared consistently on paper-and-pencil tasks before taking any action in the classroom. In examining the role of the teacher, other ways to deal with errors will be illustrated.

5. Recently, there has been growing interest in the role that metacognition plays in learning mathematics or in solving problems. Garofalo and Lester (1985) clearly point to the lack of metacognitive research in mathematics education at the time that they wrote this state-of-the-art paper. Drawing from the research in reading, special education, and memory development as well as from the problem-solving work in mathematics education, they propose the framework for problem solving shown in Figure 6.1.

Those familiar with Polya's (1945) model of problem solving will recognize the cognitive aspects: orientation, organization, execution, and verification, or as loosely translated in many elementary mathematics series: read, plan, do, and check. While the last interpretation is a gross simplification of even Polya's model, the addition of key metacognitive decisions (e.g., assessment of level of difficulty, evaluation of the adequacy of representation) may assist not only in the study of thinking necessary to solve problems but also in guiding students to be aware of their thoughts and to monitor their progress.

6. The recent interest in metacognition has brought to our attention again the need to examine learners' beliefs about mathematics and about themselves.

116

Figure 6.1. Cognitive-Metacognitive Framework

Orientation: Strategic Behavior to Assess and Understand a Problem
A. Comprehension strategies
B. Analysis of information and conditions
C. Assessment of familiarity with task
D. Initial and subsequent representations
E. Assessment of level of difficulty and chances of success

Organization: Planning of Behavior and Choice of Actions
A. Identificaton of goals and subgoals
B. Global planning
C. Local planning (to implement global plans)

Execution: Regulation of Behavior to Conform to Plans
A. Performance of local actions
B. Monitoring of progress of local and global plans
C. Trade-off decisions (e.g., speed vs accuracy, degree of elegance)

Verification: Evaluation of Decisions Made and of Outcomes of Executive Plans
A. Evaluation of orientation and organization
   1. Adequacy of representation
   2. Adequacy of organizational decisions
   3. Consistency of local plans with global plans
   4. Consistency of global plans with goals
B. Evaluation of execution
   1. Adequacy of performance of actions
   2. Consistency of actions with plans
   3. Consistency of local results with plans and problem conditions
   4. Consistency of final results with problem conditions

(From Garofalo and Lester 1985)

Schoenfeld (1985b, p. 372) conjectures that the following beliefs may present major stumbling blocks to success in mathematics:

Belief 1: Formal mathematics has little or nothing to do with real thinking or problem solving. *Corollary:* Ignore it when you need to solve problems.

Belief 2: Mathematics problems are always solved in less than ten minutes, if they are solved at all. *Corollary:* Give up after ten minutes.

Belief 3: Only geniuses are capable of discovering or creating mathematics. *First corollary:* If you forget something, too bad. After all, you're not a genius and you won't be able to derive it on your own. *Second corollary:* Accept procedures at face value, and don't try to understand why they work. After all, they are derived knowledge passed on "from above."

Although Schoenfeld describes these as conjectures, all mathematics teachers probably have anecdotes that would lend credence to these beliefs. How many times have you heard: "Why do we have to learn this? We never use it." One of the most common concerns of teachers with whom I have worked is the lack of persistence of their students in solving problems. Many teachers put the blame for lack of persistence on television, but we may need to realize that students have had many years of experience in solving problems (or doing exercises) that required far less than ten minutes apiece. No wonder students have the belief that immediacy is a goal in mathematics.

One anecdote related to the third belief gives me hope for help in overcoming such attitudes. Recently, while working with a school system that was using *Developing Mathematical Processes* (DMP) (Romberg, Harvey, Moser, and Montgomery 1974-76), a teacher told me her experience. Having a strong interest in language arts and not much in mathematics, she decided to be a pilot teacher when her district was selecting programs, so that when the decision was to be made, she could speak against this demanding program. To make a long story short, she saw what was happening to the children in DMP and it fit with her conception of developing language arts. She soon became a resource teacher for the program's implementation in the district. At the time I met her, she had been somewhat concerned about her mathematics background and working with the upper-grade teachers. Then, she had one of those rare occasions in real life when she had to use fractions. Her immediate reaction was to panic, but she stopped and asked herself, "What would they do in DMP?" She was able to generalize from approaches used in the early grades of DMP to solve her problem. Until then, she had never realized that she could figure out something that she had forgotten. How many students get through school and college feeling this way about mathematics?

There is more than conjectures and anecdotes about beliefs in the mathematics education literature; research does exist, although those who have done this research would be the first to say that there is more to be done. (Lester and Garofalo 1982, McLeod 1985.)

In summary, many of the same assumptions articulated about learning in Chapter 1 are present in the research and folklore of mathematics education. However, before looking at the implications of these for instruction, I want to point out some differences in the way mathematics education views the concept of organizational patterns from other disciplines.

Organizational Patterns

The basic premise that learning is organizing knowledge certainly is true in mathematics, and there are many examples of organizing and representing or modeling knowledge in this chapter. However, we must be cautious in thinking that this organization is parallel to that in other disciplines. To try to impose generic organizational patterns upon a discipline already structured would be counterproductive. This is similar to applying general laws of learning to mathematics. As some psychologists have come to realize:

> For many decades mathematicians and educators committed to improving the intellectual power of mathematics instruction were unable to find much interest in the works of psychologists. This is not surprising, for psychologists—if they attended to mathematics at all—generally were attempting to make mathematical subjects fit general laws of learning rather than trying to understand the processes of mathematics in particular. This is now changing (Resnick and Ford 1981, p.v.).

Thus, if we are to progress in understanding how structure affects the learning of mathematics, we must take into consideration the mathematical structure. Silver (1979) found that capable problem solvers focus on the essential structure of the problem while less capable students focus on many irrelevant details. Capable problem solvers also organize their knowledge in large chunks on the basis of fundamental mathematical structures (Carpenter 1985c, p. 58). There is also evidence that children impose structure on mathematics. Look at the structure the young children imposed upon the problems cited on page 113. Our job as teachers is to help them organize this structure into larger chunks. In this case, we need to help them understand that both of these problems may be solved by subtraction.

It is important to keep the idiosyncratic nature of mathematics in mind and not to neglect structure, but to use the structure of mathematics and the structure that children naturally impose upon it.

Teaching

Probably because much of the research on teaching and instruction has been done by generalists, there is a common base from which to begin. In general, the role of the teacher and the concepts of strategic teaching cut across disciplines, including the mathematics discipline. The content drives the instruction, however, when one considers specific strategies for particular parts of mathematics. Let us look at the three topics: the role of the teacher, specific strategies, and concepts of strategic teaching.

The role of the teacher. Through the years there have been many attempts to deliver instruction in a meaningful manner; that is, in a way that captures some of the aspects proposed in this book. Peck and his associates (1980) found that children had no way to link the process of adding fractions to anything meaningful and no way to decide if an answer was reasonable. They instituted the strategy of "How can you tell?" with a strong emphasis on physical and pictorial models or representations of text. The role of the instructor was to define the symbols, help children link the symbols to the concrete experiences, and to focus attention on ways children could make correct decisions for themselves. The teacher was both a questioner and a doubter, not a source of immediate reinforcement.

One of the processes in DMP (Romberg et al. 1974-76) was that of validating. The teacher was encouraged to have students show or tell how they solved problems whether the answer was correct or not. In classes where students were expected to validate, there was soon an air of confidence. There was no grabbing the eraser or blank stare when the teacher asked a student how he or she did something. Instead, the teacher often got a minilesson from the child along with the look of "Boy, you must be dumb." Certainly, good teachers have used questioning techniques that have required students to think, such as those recommended by Burns (1985) and Johnson (1982).

A current project and one that fits closely with the aims of teaching thinking is the Cognitively Guided Instruction (CGI) project (Fennema, Carpenter, and Peterson 1986, p. 16). Fennema and colleagues are investigating the translation of cognitive and instructional science into educational practice and evaluating its effectiveness. Five guiding principles have been set:

1. Instructional decisions should be based on what is known about each child's cognition and knowledge.

2. Instruction should be organized to involve children mentally and enable each child to construct and understand knowledge.

3. Instruction should stress the relationships among concepts, problem solving, and skills.

4. Classrooms should be organized so that children are mentally involved, gain understandings, and so that teachers can assess children's cognition and knowledge.

5. Instruction should encourage children's monitoring of their own thinking and accepting responsibility for their own learning.

The emphasis of their CGI model is on the teacher, a teacher who can affect learning. This teacher must have in-depth knowledge of children's learning and hold beliefs congruent with the guiding principles. At present, the knowledge base commonly used is that from early number work with addition and subtraction (Carpenter 1985a). The CGI model depends heavily on a well-developed structure of how children learn a given topic and on the ability of the teacher to assess the knowledge of each child and provide appropriate experiences. In this way, it is content-driven. Although the general principles may hold for any mathematical topic, it will require a more sophisticated understanding of learning before CGI can be used with most topics.

Certainly the CGI model calls for the teacher to be a mediator, a manager, and an executive. It also contains aspects of the apprentice model as it encourages children to accept more responsibility for their own learning.

Specific strategies. Although metacognitive strategies are generally common to all disciplines, certain strategies interact with the task and thus become specific to mathematics. For example, if children believe that problems with larger numbers are more difficult even with a calculator, that belief will influence their success.

On the other hand, cognitive strategies are usually tied closely to the content. As stated previously, we are still learning what many of these are, how children process information, and how they make connections. Thus, it is premature to outline specific strategies for the teacher to follow as these relate to specific content. The planning section below attempts, however, to outline some general instructional strategies and to illustrate them with examples for conceptual learning, procedural learning, and problem solving.

Concepts of strategic teaching. The concepts of explicit teaching, misconceptions, scaffolding, and phases of learning have their counterparts in mathematics education. As alluded to previously, there is research on *explicit teaching of strategies* in mathematics. In particular, the teaching of the "thinking strategies for facts" (Steinberg 1985, Thornton et al. 1983) is illustrative of strategies that help in procedural learning. The problem-solving literature gives evidence that teaching strategies improve performance, and yet they are not the entire answer for successful problem solving.

We know that students have many *misconceptions.* There is not much research on instruction that addresses these misconceptions directly. There are models of instruction (Good, Grouws, and Ebmeier 1983), however, that try to suggest ways teachers can be aware of misconceptions earlier and take steps to prevent their solidification.

The problem-solving approaches probably come the closest to advocating the principles underlying the concept of *scaffolding.* From the modeling of problem solving so masterfully done by Polya (1985) to recommendations for small-group work, one finds examples of these principles. Collins, Brown, and Newman (in press) used Schoenfeld's work as an illustration of apprenticeship in mathematics.

The *three phases of instruction* have been most explicitly described by Lester and his associates (Garofalo and Lester 1985). As in the language arts areas, these phases were based on knowledge of how expert problem solvers think while solving problems. For example, they spend more time in the after phase, not only checking their answer but reflecting on the other evaluation aspects.

The Planning Guide for Strategic Teaching in Mathematics, at the end of the chapter, incorporates the ideas from both problem-solving models in Figure 6.1 with the generic Planning Guide for Strategic Thinking in Chapter 2. It also considers aspects of concepts and procedures, since they also can encourage thinking.

Applications of the Mathematics Planning Guide

Three examples follow that illustrate teaching skills to third graders, concepts to eighth graders, and problem solving to secondary students. These are not intended to be full lesson plans or transcripts of lessons, but suggestions of how the planning guide can be used in different areas and at different levels.

SKILLS INSTRUCTION

Much of mathematics instruction currently is focused on skills or procedural knowledge and much of the instruction is done in a rote, mechanistic manner. Thinking is encouraged very little, and an unbalanced curriculum evolves that neglects concepts and problem solving. The Planning Guide for Strategic Teaching in Mathematics (see page 132) can help us focus our teaching of procedural knowledge to enhance thinking and to include some conceptual and conditional knowledge even in procedural instruction.

Let us look at an example of teaching a procedure or algorithm for subtracting three-digit numbers to third graders. First, we will assume that they are ready for this topic as they are well on their way to mastering two-digit subtraction and concepts related to three-digit numeration. Second, we will assume that they are accustomed to this type of teaching and have been introduced to many additive and subtractive situations. The first assumption is realistic, but the second is probably questionable, albeit desirable, in many classes.

Preparing for Learning

This phase, for this example, may be considered as preparation for the presentation of the three-digit algorithm. It is in this phase that we set the scene for what will be learned and why it is being learned, activate past knowledge, and focus direction and interest.

Preview problem. Present the following type of problem based on data gathered from your students.

Jane has sold 25 boxes of Girl Scout Cookies. Her goal is to sell 42 boxes. How many more boxes does she need to sell in order to reach her goal?

Remember that this is not a new problem situation for the class, but one that we are using to set the scene and to activate background knowledge.

Activate background knowledge. Ask questions such as the following:

> What is Jane's goal?
> Has she met this goal?
> Is she near her goal?
> Can anyone draw a picture to represent this problem?
> (Expect a drawing such as the following.)

What do we need to find?
How do we find the other part if we know how many in all and one part?
Can anyone think of another way to solve this problem?
Why would Jane want to know how many more?

Be aware of misconceptions; some children may think they need to add the two numbers since this is an additive situation to many students. (25 plus what is 42?) Raise the question of why 25 + 42 is not reasonable (it is more than her goal).

Have the children solve the problem by subtraction, 42 − 25. Hit the misconception of reversals head on by asking about this exercise.

$$\begin{array}{r} 42 \\ -\underline{25} \end{array}$$ WHAT IS WRONG HERE?
SHOW ME WHY.

Review here that there are not enough ones (2) to take 5 away.

Focus direction. Move to the objective of three-digit subtraction by changing the above problem as follows:

> Jane and her friends sold **325** boxes of Girl Scout Cookies. Their goal is to sell **642** boxes. How many more boxes do they need to sell in order to reach their goal?

Compare this problem to its original version by asking what has changed (who sold, how many were sold, and goal). Work toward setting up the subtraction problem:

$$\begin{array}{r} 642 \\ -\underline{325} \end{array}$$

Discuss goal. At this point (notice it was not done at the beginning of the lesson) let the children know that the goal is to extend their skills from two-digit subtraction to three-digit subtraction.

Presenting the Content

Pause/reflect. Ask the children if they know how to do the three-digit subtraction. Contrast the two examples:

$$642 \qquad 42$$
$$-325 \qquad -25$$

Ask how they are alike and different. Encourage the children to realize that they already know how to subtract the ones and tens in both—and probably they will be able to figure out the hundreds! Have the children validate their answer with power-10 blocks.

Initiate action. Continue with other examples such as

$$524$$
$$-391$$

This example brings in the new part of the algorithm. Here the ones do not have to be regrouped, but the tens do. Ask the children what they would do. Encourage the use of models or representations—at least the generalization, "I need more tens in the tens' place."

Assimilate ideas. It may take several days to present different examples and provide enough practice. Do not forget to keep the different additive and subtractive situations and discussion in these lessons also. At some point, have the children contrast how the following exercises are alike and different:

A. 418   B. 481   *We start with ones, same digits, different*
  − 253   − 253   *places. In A, we regroup tens; in B, ones.*

C. 346   D. 246   *I have to regroup ones in C and both in D.*
  − 128   − 178

Applying/Integrating

Integrate/organize. At the close of each lesson, have the children share what they have learned and how they would use the knowledge. Also have them tell which exercises seem to be more difficult and why, as well as what helps them with these. Keep the link between the problems in the forefront of their thinking.

CONCEPTS INSTRUCTION

Let us apply the Mathematics Planning Guide to teaching conceptual knowledge. In this example, we will examine the rhombus, its properties, and relationships to other quadrilaterals. We will assume that the eighth graders are familiar with parallelograms, rectangles, squares and their properties. In fact, some quadrilaterals may be recognized as rhombuses.

Preparing for Learning

Discuss the goal. Let the students know they are going to add one more special quadrilateral, the rhombus, to their knowledge of polygons.

Preview problem. Elicit what there may be to learn about the rhombus and generate a list of general questions and properties. (See Figure 6.2.)

Activate background. To assist with generating the list of properties, have students list the things they know about squares, rectangles, and parallelograms.

Figure 6.2. Quadrilaterals

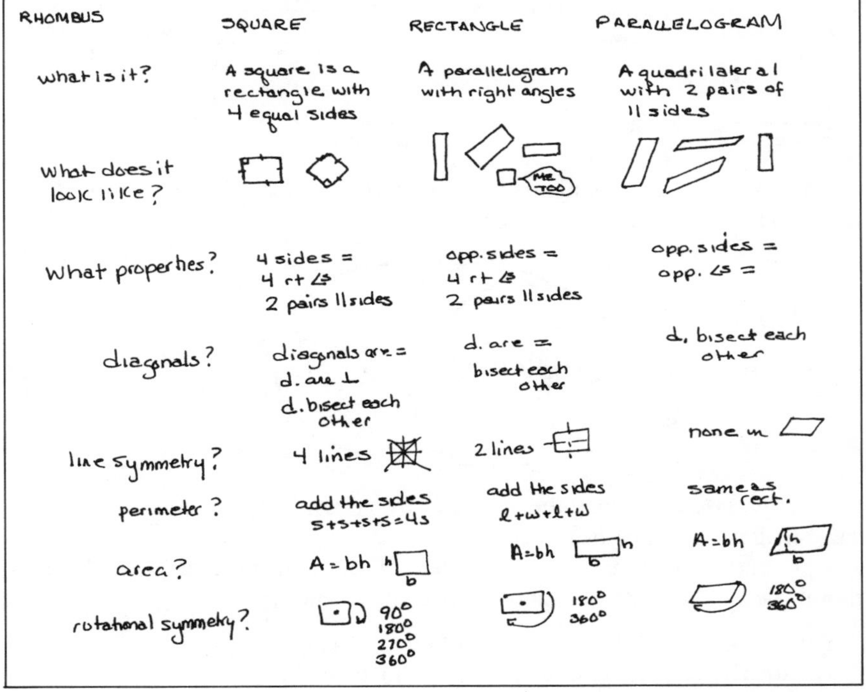

Presenting the Content

Focus direction. Show these sketches:

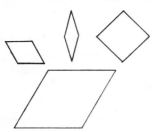
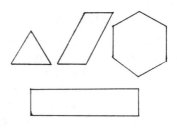

Pause/reflect. Examine the examples and nonexamples of rhombuses. After asking what characterizes the rhombus and why each nonexample is not a rhombus, develop a definition of the rhombus.

Discuss whether all squares are rhombuses, and whether all rhombuses are squares.

Help the students establish the relationship that all squares are rhombuses, but not vice versa. Consider this representation:

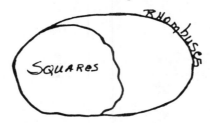

Initiate action. Once the students are convinced of what a rhombus is, have small groups investigate its properties, especially symmetry, perimeter, diagonals, and area. Have each small group of four students make four different rhombuses and answer questions such as the following:

Do all rhombuses have diagonals of equal length?
Do any rhombuses have diagonals of equal length?
How many lines of symmetry does a rhombus have?

If you cut a rhombus on its diagonals, what do you discover?
How can you find the area of a rhombus?

Monitor progress and give hints as necessary. Encourage children to make their own discoveries.

Assimilate ideas. Have the small groups report their findings, telling how they arrived at these. Also, have them discuss any questions that arose in their groups.

Applying/Integrating

Integrate/organize. Look again at the relationships between the properties of these four quadrilaterals: How are squares like rhombuses, how are rhombuses like parallelograms, how are rectangles different from squares? Help the students see that all squares are rhombuses and all squares are rectangles and all squares, rhombuses, and rectangles are parallelograms. A diagram like the following may help organize the information.

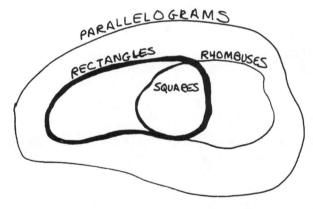

Extend learning. Some children may need the challenge of investigating trapezoids and kites.

PROBLEM-SOLVING INSTRUCTION

Let us look at an example of using the planning guide with a problem presented to a secondary geometry class. The problem and hints are adapted from Milauskas (1987).

Preparing for Learning

We will assume that we have assessed the level of the learners and that they have the prerequisite knowledge—area of triangles and parallelograms and similarity of triangles—as well as experience with problem-solving strategies such as examining a subproblem, taking a special case, and modeling the problem.

Preview problem. Present the following problem: The area of a parallelogram is 60. A segment is drawn from one vertex to the midpoint of an opposite side. The diagonal is drawn between the other two vertices. Find the area of the four regions formed.

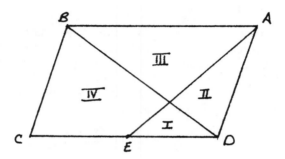

At this point, ask questions to ascertain whether the students understand the problem:

What do you know about this parallelogram?

How were the lines inside the parallelogram drawn?

What are we to find?

Activate prior knowledge. Make a list of things that might help in solving this problem by brainstorming. Students may give a list such as the one that follows, or you may need to prompt them with leading questions.

$$A = bh$$
E is the midpoint of CD.
Area I + Area IV = 30
Area I + Area II = 15
$$ED = \tfrac{1}{2}b$$
Sum of all the region's area is 60
Area II + Area III = 30

At this point, some students may think the base is 10 and the altitude is 6. You would need to confront this misconception, possibly by drawing the following figure and asking whether it satisfies the conditions of the problem.

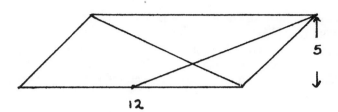

Or you may want to capitalize on the idea that these are special cases of the problem, and that solving the special case may help us generalize to the original problem.

Focus direction/interest. If the discussion has proceeded along this path, you would realize that one of the keys to solving this problem has not been found. (The fact that triangles I and III are similar.) Often our temptation is to tell the students this, but we need to let them wrestle with the problem. After forming small groups, you might suggest the following for any group that may need more direction:

1. Try a special case—maybe a rectangle or a particular parallelogram whose area is 60.

2. Draw a parallelogram to scale and see what you note.

3. We are missing a key relationship between two of the triangles (much more directive).

Preparing the Content

Pause/reflect. During this step you need to be as silent as you can be—let the students decide how their small group will proceed.

Initiate action. The students' progress will clue you as to needed steps in this phase. Let's suppose you find the following happening in some of the groups.

Group A—They are approaching the problem algebraically and have a "mess" of equations and unknowns as follows:

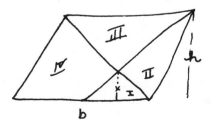

$$A_I = \tfrac{1}{2}\left(\tfrac{1}{2}b\,x\right)$$
$$A_{II} = \tfrac{1}{2}\left(\tfrac{1}{2}bh\right) - \tfrac{1}{2}\cdot\tfrac{1}{2}bx$$
$$A_{III} = \tfrac{1}{2}(h-x)\,\tfrac{b}{2}$$
$$A_{IV} = \tfrac{1}{2}bh - \tfrac{1}{2}\cdot\tfrac{1}{2}b\,x$$

You need to help them see how x is related to h, but encourage them to follow through with their plan.

Group B—This group is sitting with apparently little done and with no clear idea of how to proceed. Give each of the four a copy of a parallelogram as shown and let them cut out the areas and suggest that they try to see how I and III are related.

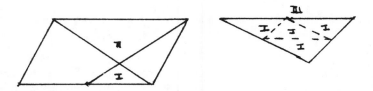

Group C—This group has realized that the two triangles are similar, but think that the area of III is twice as large as the area of I since the lengths are in this proportion. Redirect their thoughts.

Assimilate ideas. Group C proceeded with the last hint and found a solution. You might want to challenge them with the following extension.

M and N are trisection points

Group A have tangled themselves into a long equation. Refocus them to simplify things earlier.

$$A_I + A_{II} + A_{III} + A_{IV} = \tfrac{1}{4}bx + \tfrac{1}{4}bh - \tfrac{1}{4}bx + \tfrac{1}{4}(h-x) +$$
$$\tfrac{1}{2}bh - \tfrac{1}{4}bx$$
$$\text{But, } x = \tfrac{1}{3}h.$$

Of course, there will be other questions from other groups, but at this point you may also want some of the students in Group C or Group A to assist the other groups. Encourage those students not to tell how, but to work with the group on their plan.

Applying/Integrating

Integrate/organize. At this stage, have the students share solutions and approaches to the problem.

Assess achievement. Discuss with the groups how the different approaches were alike, and which they were more comfortable with.

Extend learning. Here are a couple more extensions that you might have available.

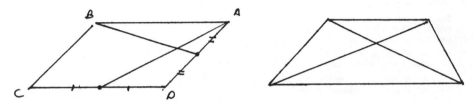

Adaptations to Low and High Achievers

Capable students simplify the learning of mathematics by imposing structure, seeing the "big picture," and reflecting on their thinking, while less capable students learn isolated facts and thus have more to learn and less chance of using their knowledge. Studies of low-achieving students do not paint a pleasant picture. Good (1986) summarizes these findings: less capable students have less conceptualization and more practice, less opportunity to think, less autonomy, less opportunity for self-evaluation, less honest and contingent feedback, and receive less respect as individual learners with unique interests and needs. Thus, the less capable student has little chance of developing strong cognitive strategies and probably even less chance of developing megacognitive strategies.

On the other hand, this chapter began with the denouncement of the lack of thinking in mathematics classes. This was for all students—even the most capable. My position at this point is not to make adaptations for either group. If the tenets of cognitive instruction and strategic teaching are followed, all students will benefit. If, after a fair trial of this type of instruction it is shown that the needs of either the low- or the high-achieving students are not being met, then it will be time to readdress this issue.

Closing Remarks

The main assumption of this analysis is that thinking enhances students' ability to learn and use mathematics in a meaningful manner. It is hoped that taking this perspective is not antithetical to the noble goal of Polya (1983) that we should teach thinking in mathematics to improve the mind, or to improve thinking itself.

Planning Guide for Strategic Teaching in Mathematics

PREPARING THE CONTENT

Assess level of learner
set expectations

Discuss goal
discuss nature of task
model/elicit criteria for success

Preview problem/learning experience
model/guide preview (e.g., examine pictorial clues/content)

Activate background knowledge
elicit background concepts and procedures
confront misconceptions
elicit strategies and plans

Focus direction/interest
provide hints or structured activities
model interest and clarify purpose

PRESENTING THE CONTENT

Pause/reflect
model/guide planning
elicit/discuss faulty logic, contraditions

Initiate action
monitor progress (give hints if necessary)

Assimilate ideas
discuss progress, change direction if necessary,
give extension
guide articulation process

APPLYING/INTEGRATING

Integrate/organize
share and discuss solutions and execution
compare to "model" solutions and other learning experiences

Assess achievement
model and discuss evaluation
discuss old misconceptions
provide reinforcement

Extend learning
provide extensions of increased diversity and complexity
discuss growth

References

Brown, J. S., and R. R. Burton. "Diagnostic Models for Procedural Bugs in Basic Mathematical Skills." *Cognitive Science* 2 (1978): 153-192.
Burns, M. "The Role of Questioning." *Arithmetic Teacher* 32, 6 (1985): 14-17.

Carpenter, T. P. "Review of *Children's Counting Types: Philosophy, Theory, and Application* by L. P. Steffe, E. von Glasersfeld, J. Richards, and P. Cobb." *Journal for Research in Mathematics Education* 16 (1985a): 70-76.

Carpenter, T. P. "Learning to Add and Subtract: An Exercise in Problem Solving." In *Teaching and Learning Mathematical Problem Solving: Multiple Research Perspectives*, edited by E. A. Silver. Hillsdale, N.J.: Erlbaum, 1985b, 17-40.

Carpenter, T. P. "Research on the Role of Structure in Thinking." *Arithmetic Teacher* 32, 6 (1985c): 58-60.

Carpenter, T. P., M. K. Corbitt, H. S. Kepner, M. M. Lindquist, and R. E. Reys. *Results from the Second Mathematics Assessment of the National Assessment of Educational Progress*. Reston, Va.: National Council of Teachers of Mathematics, 1981.

Collins, A., J. S. Brown, and S. Newman. "Cognitive Apprenticeship: Teaching Students the Craft of Reading, Writing, and Mathematics." In *Cognition and Instruction: Issues and Agendas*, edited by L. B. Resnick. Hillsdale, N.J.: Erlbaum, in press.

Davis, R. B. *Learning Mathematics: The Cognitive Science Approach to Mathematics Education*. Norwood, N.J.: Ablex Publishing, 1984.

Fennema, E., T. P. Carpenter, and P. L. Peterson. "Teachers' Decision Making and Cognitively Guided Instruction: A New Paradigm for Curriculum Development." Paper presented at the Tenth Annual Psychology of Mathematics Education Conference, London, 1986.

Fischbein, E., M. Deri, M. S. Nello, and M. S. Marino. "The Role of Implicit Models in Solving Verbal Problems in Multiplication and Division." *Journal for Research in Mathematics Education* 16 (1985): 3-17.

Fuys, D., D. Geddes, and R. Tischler, eds. *English Translation of Selected Writings of Dina van Hiele-Geldof and Pierre M. van Hiele*. New York: Brooklyn College, School of Education, 1984.

Garofalo, J., and F. K. Lester. "Metacognition, Cognitive Monitoring, and Mathematical Performance." *Journal for Research in Mathematics Education* 16 (1985): 163-176.

Good, T. L. "Improving Development Lessons in Mathematics by Changing Teachers' Views of Mathematics and Their Instructional Practices." In *A Change in Emphasis*, edited by R. Lodholz. St. Louis: Parkway Schools, 1986.

Good, T. L., G. A. Grouws, and H. Ebmeier. *Active Mathematics Teaching*. New York: Longman, 1983.

Hiebert, J. "Children's Mathematical Learning: The Struggle to Link Form and Understanding." *Elementary School Journal* 84 (1984): 497-513.

Johnson, D. R. *Every Minute Counts*. Palo Alto, Calif.: Dale Seymour Publications, 1982.

Kilpatrick, J. "Stop the Bandwagon, I Want Off." *Arithmetic Teacher* 28 (1981): 2.

Kilpatrick, J. "Reflection and Recursion." In *Proceeding to the Fifth International Congress on Mathematical Education*, edited by M. Carss. Boston: Birkhauser, 1986.

Lesh, R., and M. Landau, eds. *Acquisition of Mathematical Concepts and Processes*. New York: Academic Press, 1983.

Lester, F. K., and J. Garofalo. "Metacognitive Aspects of Elementary School Students' Performance on Arithmetic Tasks." Paper presented at the meeting of the American Educational Research Association, New York, 1982.

Lindquist, M. M. "The Elementary School Mathematics Curriculum: Issues for Today." *Elementary School Journal* 84 (1984): 595-608.

McLeod, D. B. "Affective Issues in Research on Teaching Mathematical Problem Solving." In *Teaching and Learning Mathematical Problem Solving, Multiple Research Perspective*, edited by E. A. Silver. Hillsdale, N.J.: Erlbaum, 1985, 267-279.

Milauskas, G. B. "Creative Geometry Problems Can Lead to Creative Problem Solvers." In *Learning and Teaching Geometry, K-12, 1987 Yearbook*, edited by M. M. Lindquist. Reston, Va.: National Council of Teachers of Mathematics, 1987, 69-84.

National Assessment of Educational Progress. *The Third National Mathematics Assessment: Results, Trends and Issues*. Denver: Education Commission of the States, 1983.

National Council of Teachers of Mathematics (NCTM). *An Agenda for Action: Recommendations for School Mathematics of the 1980s*. Reston, Va.: NCTM, 1980.

Peck, D. M., S. M. Jencks, and L. J. Chatterly. "How Can You Tell?" *Elementary School Journal* 80 (1980): 178-184.

Polya, G. *How to Solve It*. Princeton, N.J.: Princeton University Press, 1945.

Polya, G. "Mathematics Promotes the Mind." In *Proceedings from the Fourth International Congress of Mathematics Education*, edited by M. Zweng, T. Green, J. Kilpatrick, H. Pollak, and M. Suydam. Boston: Birkhauser, 1983.

Resnick, L. B., and W. W. Ford. *The Psychology of Mathematics Instruction*. Hillsdale, N.J.: Erlbaum, 1981.

Romberg, T. A., and T. P. Carpenter. "Research on Teaching and Learning." In *The Third Handbook of Research on Teaching*, edited by M. C. Wittrock. New York: Macmillan, 1986, 850-873.

Romberg, T. A., J. G. Harvey, J. M. Moser, and M. E. Montgomery. *Developing Mathematical Processes*. Chicago: Rand McNally, 1974-1976.

Schoenfeld, A. H. *Mathematical Problem Solving*. New York: Academic Press, 1985a.

Schoenfeld, A. H. "Metacognitive and Epistemological Issues in Mathematical Understanding." In *Teaching and Learning Mathematical Problem Solving: Multiple Research Perspectives*, edited by E. A. Silver. Hillsdale, N.J.: Erlbaum, 1985b, 361-379.

Shaughnessy, M. "Problem-solving Derailers: The Influence of Misconceptions on Problem-solving Performance." In *Teaching and Learning Mathematical Problem Solving: Multiple Research Perspectives*, edited by E. A. Silver. Hillsdale, N.J.: Erlbaum, 1985, 399-415.

Silver, E. A. "Student Perceptions of Relatedness Around Mathematical Verbal Problems." *Journal for Research in Mathematics Education* 10 (1979): 195-210.

Silver, E. A. *Teaching and Learning Mathematical Problem Solving: Multiple Research Perspectives*. Hillsdale, N.J.: Erlbaum, 1985.

Skemp, R. R. "Relational Understanding and Instrumental Understanding." *Arithmetic Teacher* 26, 3 (1978): 9-15.

Steinberg, R. M. "Instruction on Derived Fact Strategies in Addition and Subtraction." *Journal for Research in Mathematics Education* 16 (1985): 337-355.

Thornton, C. A., G. A. Jones, and M. A. Toohey. "A Multisensory Approach to Thinking Strategies for Remedial Instruction in Basic Addition Facts." *Journal for Research in Mathematical Education* 14 (1983): 193-203.

Richard Beach

7

Strategic
Teaching in
Literature

I magine three hypothetical secondary students, Mark, Sally, and Lynn. They are all relatively good readers, but none of them has had much experience in interpreting literature. They have just read a short story; each is responding to a different set of directions.

Mark was asked to "write a critical essay interpreting the theme of this story." He doesn't really know what to do, nor does he have any driving purpose. He has little idea of what it means to "interpret the theme." He stares at a blank sheet of paper, not knowing where to begin.

Sally is responding to a series of worksheet questions: "what is the setting," "who is the main character," "what does the tree represent," "why did the character leave at the end," and so forth. While she is able to answer these questions, she doesn't perceive her answers as adding up to anything, as really achieving any coherent understanding of the story. The short-answer questions commonly asked of students often tend to fragment rather than organize students' attempts to formulate hypotheses or ideas about a text (Marshall 1984). Moreover, because she assumes that there are "correct answers," she doesn't feel much ownership in her responses.

Lynn is responding to a series of guided activities, designed, she is told, to help her explain a character's actions in the story. The first activity asks her to list some of the character's behaviors. Next, she is asked to associate beliefs and goals typically associated with those behaviors. She then thinks about some related experiences in her own life, along with associated beliefs and goals, and about how she used those beliefs and goals to explain her own behavior. Finally, she links her own explanation of the actions to the text to explain the character's actions.

In contrast to Mark, Lynn has some sense of direction. Each activity builds on previous activities in a sequential manner, "first things first." Moreover, she has some sense of how each activity contributes to achieving the overall purpose of explaining the character's action. Activities designed to help students define relationships or adopt different perspectives may encourage a reflective orientation conducive to formulating hypotheses or ideas (Applebee 1986).

Unlike Sally, Lynn knows that there are no "correct answers." This enhances her ownership of her responses. And, from responding to these activities, Lynn is learning a systematic way of exploring ideas—a set of heuristics for interpreting texts.

In this chapter, I describe a strategically oriented approach to teaching literature through the use of *guided response activities* in which students respond to a literary text according to a series of sequential activities. These activities are based on using a range of different response strategies—engaging, connecting, describing/exploring, interpreting, and judging. These activities differ from answering traditional worksheet or textbook questions in that students are continually relating their inferences to an emerging hypothesis or set of ideas. Because the inference strategies are organized according to certain heuristic patterns, students are incidentally learning a set of heuristics for exploring and extending their responses to a literary work. For example, by initially describing their perceptions of a poem, then connecting those perceptions to their own autobiographical experiences, and then using those experiences to interpret the poem, a student is learning to employ a *describe/ connect/interpret* heuristic (Bleich 1981, Petrosky 1982). Guided activities include not only writing but also discussion, debate, oral interpretation, role play, creative writing, or media productions.

Simply asking students to "just respond" to texts is, as was the case with Mark, insufficient. In order to interpret a text, most students may need more guidance or *scaffolding* (Applebee and Langer 1984) for generating and extending their responses. The describe/connect/interpret heuristic serves as a scaffold for enhancing interpretation. Or, students could think about a key event in a text—the breakup of a marriage—in terms of characters' knowledge or beliefs about each other, their goals or motives, and their own personality attributes. Once students become accustomed to explaining characters' acts in terms of knowledge/beliefs, goals/motives, and attributes/categories, they may automatically apply these perspectives to any explanation, possibly enhancing the depth of that explanation. And, as students learn to apply the structure provided by the guided activity intuitively, teachers can encourage more autonomous responses in students' writing, journals, small-group discussions, or extended essays.

The remainder of this chapter is divided into four sections. The first is a description of guided activites: their goals and uses, specific inference strategies, specific response strategies, techniques to extend responses, and distinguishing features of guided response activities. The second is a brief section on evaluating students' literary responses. The third section offers an extended example showing how to devise guided activities for a specific poem. And the final section discusses the benefits of guided activities.

Guided Activities

Goals/Uses of Guided Activities

Linking Students' Experience to the Text. Guided activities help students learn to draw on their prior knowledge (Langer 1984) or autobiographical experience (Petrosky 1982) in making inferences. By connecting related knowledge or experiences to a text, students can activate schema that help them better understand the text. For example, by comparing a mystery story to previous mystery stories, students may perceive certain characteristic hero attributes.

At the same time, in order to suspend their disbelief and "enter" the world of the text, students also need to learn to recognize the difference between their own experience or world view and the experience or "world" portrayed in the text (Galda 1982, Jacobsen 1982). In transporting themselves into another world, students experience different social, cultural, and economic perspectives, which helps them perceive the limitations of their own social and cultural attitudes and world view. From these experiences, students learn to apply the prior knowledge most relevant to understanding a text selectively, for example, by perceiving a text, situation, character, goal, or theme as representative of a certain type or genre—as "a mystery," "comedy," "villain," "sales pitch," "marriage ceremony," and so forth.

Using Students' Knowledge of Organizational Patterns. Additionally, teachers may use the knowledge of content and organizational patterns that students bring to a text, using frames, writing plans, and text structures as scaffolds. That is, students often have difficulty extending their thinking about texts beyond immediate, superficial responses. Frames and text structures may help students focus attention on important structural elements of a text and direct their thinking according to a logical plan or scaffold (Applebee and Langer 1984; Bracewell, Fredriksen, and Fredriksen 1982).

Unfortunately, teacher discussion and worksheet or textbook questions often are unrelated, each focusing on different aspects of a text. For example, after answering questions about characters' acts, students may be asked to think about their beliefs or goals, without necessarily perceiving any relationship between these acts, beliefs, or goals. If these questions were related in a more systematic manner around an *act/belief/goal* frame or scaffold, students could learn how to relate these elements in order to explain a character's act.

Students could also learn to extend and organize their responses according to certain text structures: *opinion/example, cause/effect, problem/solution*, and so forth (Meyer 1975, Jones 1985). For example, by applying a *problem/solution* structure, students may first define a certain problem a character faces, then explain reasons for that problem, propose possible solutions, and explain why those solutions may solve the problem.

Teachers may use these frames, scaffolds, or text structures to organize or sequence strategies in a guided activity. For example, using a sequential structure to describe what happened in the text, a student could connect that description to his or her own autobiographical experience, and then use inferences about that experience to interpret the text. Or, students may list characteristics of different characters and then contrast or compare the characters according to the listed characteristics using a *comparison/contrast* text structure.

Making Inferences from Text. A third goal or function of guided assignments is to help students make inferences about what I am calling *elements* from fiction and nonfiction texts. Figure 7.1 identifies these elements.

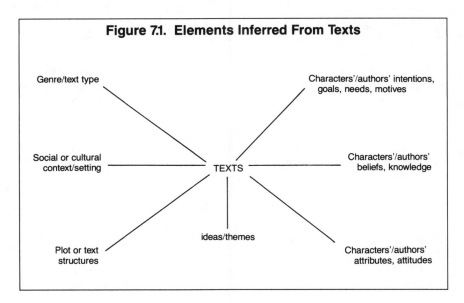

Figure 7.1. Elements Inferred From Texts

Genre/text type

Characters'/authors' intentions, goals, needs, motives

Social or cultural context/setting

TEXTS

Characters'/authors' beliefs, knowledge

Plot or text structures

ideas/themes

Characters'/authors' attributes, attitudes

Interpreting texts requires a reader to go beyond the text in order to infer the text's genre or type, setting, context, plot, ideas or a character's or author/narrator's intentions, goals, needs, motives, beliefs, knowledge, attributes, or attitudes. In order to infer these elements, readers employ inference strategies such as engaging, associating, and describing. In order to construct guided activities, teachers need to understand how readers use certain strategies to infer these elements (Iser 1978, Culler 1975, Beach and Appleman 1984). All of this stems from the idea that the meaning of language depends upon its use or function; interpreting the meaning involves defining how a character, narrator, or author is using language.

For example, one of the most basic strategies involves explaining a character's actions (in terms of one or more of these elements: goals, needs, beliefs, knowledge, attributes, etc.). To take one episode: in the beginning of a story, Mary says to Sally:

"There's a good movie coming to town this Friday."

Sally replies, "That's nice."

This exchange involves a series of ambiguous speech acts. A reader may infer that Mary is inviting Sally to go to the movie or simply stating the fact that a movie is coming to town. Sally may be accepting or rejecting the invitation or simply affirming Mary's perception. In order to explain these acts or sort out this ambiguity, a reader may infer what Mary knows or believes about Sally—perhaps that Sally likes her and may want to go to the movie with her—or what Sally believes about Mary—that Mary isn't very interesting and may not be a very exciting companion.

To make these inferences, readers also draw on their prior knowledge and experience. For example, readers may draw on their knowledge of their conception of "revenge" for conceiving of a series of character acts motivated by a goal. Or, in thinking about a character, they may draw on their conception of a "sidekick" based on certain character attributes such as knowledge of "the road ahead," loyalty, and willingness to deal with minor details.

In making inferences about nonfiction texts, readers draw on their knowledge of rhetorical or pragmatic strategies. For example, in responding to a letter to the editor on acid rain, a reader infers the writer's knowledge about acid rain (extensive vs. little), attitude toward acid rain (positive vs. negative), intentions or motives (to argue for stiffer legislation), attributes ("reasonable," "low-keyed"), and the context or setting ("an administration opposed to spending more money to deal with the problem").

Readers also differ in the level of abstraction by which they conceive of these elements, differences that may reflect levels of cognitive development (Beach and Wendler in press), background experience with reading literature (Svensson 1985), or the ability to read a text in terms of its point (Vipond and

Hunt 1984). Conceiving of elements in terms of "higher level" social, psychological, literary, or cultural meanings affects readers' ability to activate other related elements. Take, for example, goal inferences. Being able to make inferences about overall, long range goals—"stop opposition," "improve status"—means that readers can evoke acts, character traits, or plot structures typically associated with those goals (Shank 1982). If a reader infers that a character wants to "prove her ability to others," that reader may associate the act of "working hard" or the trait of "perseverance" with achieving that goal.

Thus, learning to interpret involves learning to use strategies at a relatively high level of abstraction. Guided assignments offer teachers a repertoire of teaching/learning strategies to help students make inferences from text.

Specific Inference Strategies

The following are some specific strategies involved in inferring elements about texts, strategies that would serve as the basis for devising guided response activities.

Explaining characters' actions. One of the most basic strategies involves explaining characters' actions. Readers explain actions by inferring characters' beliefs, attitudes, or attributes (Bruce and Rubin 1984). For example, they may explain a character's failure in school in terms of inferences about that character's attitudes or low self-concept.

A guided response activity based on an explaining strategy may ask students to list characters' actions on the left side of a page. Then, on the right side of the page, the student would list beliefs, attitudes, or attributes implied by those actions. Then, for each action, the student would list those particular beliefs, attitudes, or attributes that best explain that action.

Association. Readers are constantly making associations. Drawing on social and literary knowledge, readers associate certain meanings with elements: characters' goals, settings, genre types, etc. For example, having inferred that the setting is a city, we may associate meanings such as "dark," "busy," "congested," "dangerous," "urbane," and "evil." Some of these associations are derived from social experience: "busy," "congested," "dangerous," "urbane." Others are derived from literary experience—for example, the archetypal associations, "dark" or "evil."

Or, in abstracting characters' acts, readers also learn to associate one element with another, for example, acts, beliefs, and goals. A reader will associate a certain genre ("detective stories") with certain character goals ("solve the murder"), beliefs ("the need to maintain the family honor"), or plot structures ("revenge the attack on the family"). Readers learn to explain characters' actions in terms of their traits, beliefs, or goals by perceiving certain consistent patterns in characters' actions, patterns that imply particular traits, beliefs, or goals.

To make these associations, students draw on their prior knowledge of characteristics or attitudes associated with character, setting, or story proto-types or stereotypes. Working inductively or "bottom up," their associations may point to or imply a certain prototype. Once they have enough associations to trigger a prototype, they can work deductively or "top down," using that pro-totype to review their associations in order to confirm the validity of that pro-totype.

For example, most students have acquired a prototypical conception of "villain." As they associate certain characteristics with a character, those associ-ations may suggest that the character matches their prototype for villain— "evil," "duplicitous," "lurking," "hateful," "unscrupulous." They then take that prototype and review their associations to determine if they match the charac-teristics normally associated with that prototype.

While they are making associations about characters, they also are making associations about other elements—settings or story lines. They then use the associations for one set of elements to trigger associations for other elements. For example, once they infer that a story is a "murder mystery," they may evoke other associations for characters or settings typically associated with the genre. For example, they may infer certain associations for the detective character— "knowledgeable," "insightful," "dogged," "hard-working," "ethical."

As part of a guided response activity, students would be asked to sponta-neously list, "free-write," or visually map associations for an event in the text. They would then cluster or group these associations, defining or naming these clusters or groups as representing, for example, positive or negative aspects of a character or as representing "good" versus "evil" forces.

Connecting autobiographical and literary experiences to texts. Another important strategy involves connecting one's autobiographical or literary ex-periences to the text. As readers think about a text, they may be reminded of certain related experiences or similar texts, characters, or settings. For exam-ple, in reading the novel *The Pigman*, a student may be reminded of his or her own experience of taunting an older person. Or, in reading about Steinbeck's protrayal of a character using animal metaphors in the story "Johnny Bear," stu-dents may be reminded of Steinbeck's portrayal of Lennie in *Of Mice and Men*. Students may then use their interpretations of their own experience or of a re-lated text to enhance their interpretation of the text.

In a guided activity, a student would be asked to describe these related ex-periences in some detail, interpret that experience, and then link that interpre-tation back to the text—the describe/connect/interpret heuristic previously dis-cussed.

141

Defining Setting. Defining setting involves much more than simply identifying geographical location or place. In fact, setting consists of complex social and cultural conventions or norms constituting different social contexts or "worlds."

Readers define characters' traits, beliefs, and attitudes in terms of characters' allegiance to or rejection of those social conventions constituting setting. Characters such as Elizabeth in *Pride and Prejudice* or Pip in *Great Expectations* learn to recognize the parochialism of the different social and economic worlds they encounter. However, given students' limited exposure to different past and present social or cultural contexts, they may have difficulty defining social or cultural norms or conventions (Heath 1985).

A guided activity may begin with having students define the norms or conventions ("What's appropriate versus inappropriate?") in their own social contexts or "worlds" such as school, peer groups, family, and neighborhood. For example, within their own school, students may identify several different "worlds" or "cultures": a consumer/mass media culture, an adolescent/peer culture, a school/institutional culture, or a local community social culture. Students could then describe how their behavior differs in or is influenced by these different contexts. They could then define differences or conflicts between the different "worlds" in a text. For example, after reading S. E. Hinton's *The Outsiders*, they may compare the differences in the "worlds" of the two rival gangs representing two different social classes.

Perceiving/connecting plot structures or essay organization. Another relatively complicated process involves making inferences about plot structures or essay organization. In order to perceive relationships between events in a story, readers draw on their knowledge of familiar formulas or schema such as "rags to riches," "the Cinderella complex," "the quest/journey," and "problem/solution." In some cases, instruction in story structures (Gordon and Braun 1983) based on story grammars (Stein and Glenn 1979) or story maps (Beck, Omanson, and McKeown 1982) helps students define the relationships among story episodes. For example, a story map can be used to identify an initial problem leading to subsequent episodes and a resolution of the problem. Based on these models, Mason (1983), and Mason and Au (1986) define procedures for planning story comprehension lessons: defining an objective; previewing; dividing the text into segments; developing prior knowledge prereading questions; and posing questions involving relating, predicting, and synthesizing episodes. Students could also recall or retell stories to audiences who are not familiar with a story, followed by discussion of what aspects of the story were included or omitted (Strickland and Feeley 1985).

With more complex narratives, readers learn to develop a conceptual model of the text that helps them define and revise their expectations or predictions as they move through a text (Bruce and Rubin 1984). Thus, one of the basic strategies for inferring plot development is the ability to make predictions and give reasons for these predictions based on a review of suggestive cues in the text. As they read, students could be asked to make predictions and to cite reasons for those predictions based on a review of the text.

In reading essays, students could write summaries using the following activities suggested by Hare and Borchardt (1984): defining the point, rereading and reviewing the text to verify the point inference, writing a summary with a topic sentence, and revising the summary to eliminate redundancies and repetition.

As these examples suggest, each of these strategies involves specific inferences. For example, explaining involves listing action; inferring implied beliefs, attitudes, and attributes; and then linking these inferences to specific actions. Devising guided activities to help students learn to employ these strategies therefore involves specifying those inferences and the sequence of inferences involved in employing these strategies.

Specific Response Strategies for Guided Activities

In addition to determining the inferences involved in employing a strategy, a teacher also needs to select those response strategies most applicable for understanding a specific text (Beach and Appleman 1984). A response strategy is an activity the teacher selects for the students to express their thoughts. For example, using the categories of response types developed by Purves and Beach (1972), the following *taxonomy of response strategies* consists of five basic response strategies:

- *engaging:* defining one's emotional experience or relationship with a text;
- *connecting:* relating similar experiences, attitudes, knowledge, or other texts to the text;
- *describing:* describing the nature of characters' acts, traits, beliefs, plans, goals, or an author's use of language;
- *interpreting:* inferring, explaining, or interpreting the symbolic meaning of acts, author's intentions, characters' perspectives, themes, social norms, predictions, or difficulties in understanding the text; and
- *judging:* judging the characters or the quality of the text.

Figure 7.2 on page 156 offers a taxonomy of subcategories within these basic categories. Teachers may use this taxonomy of strategies to devise guided activities by taking the following steps:

1. Read over a text and think about the types of strategies involved in inferring certain text elements and the sequence or order in which the strategies

should be used. For example, in reading a story, I may realize that in order to understand the story, I need to be able to explain a character's final action of deciding not to rob a bank.

2. Specify the strategies involved in making that inference—in this case, explaining a character's action. By thinking about the steps my students would need to follow in order to explain a character's act, I recognize that students could first cite several reasons why the character did not rob the bank. They could then use those reasons to review the text to describe previous acts, traits, or beliefs—information that may or may not verify those reasons.

3. Select activities that would help students make these inferences, specify directions, and format the activity. I may then select certain writing activities that best help students make certain inferences—activities such as listing, jotting, free-writing, brainstorming, mapping, treeing, clustering, dialogues, journal-writing, nutshelling, questioning—activities involving "writing to learn" (Gere 1985). I would first have students list some reasons why the character did not rob the bank. For each reason listed ("he was lazy," "he didn't want to go to jail," etc.), I would have students review the story and list acts, traits, and beliefs that serve to verify that reason as valid.

4. Define a final writing activity. I would have students write their own explanation as to why the character did not rob the bank. The information developed through the listing and reviewing activities should result in explanations that contain more specific, elaborate information than if the students had simply started writing about the question, "Why did the character decide not to rob the bank?" Completing these "prewriting" activities often results in better quality final essays (Reilly, Beach, and Crabtree 1986).

Teachers may also teach these strategies by modeling or demonstrating how they used certain strategies to understand texts, constantly linking the strategies to their purposes or goals (Palincsar and Brown 1985). Once students understand how to employ these strategies, teachers then encourage students to formulate their own questions, lead discussions, or tutor peers, an approach that results in improved comprehension (Brown and Palincsar 1982).

Techniques to Extend Responses

Ultimately, students need to learn to interpret texts without the assistance of guided activities. As students acquire certain strategies of heuristics from completing guided response tasks, they may apply their acquired heuristics to some of the following forms of unstructured, open-ended talk and writing about literature, reducing their dependency on the guided activities.

Journal or essay writing. A central element in open-ended journal or essay writing is that students have a sense of ownership in articulating their ideas.

144

Rather than restating or recasting information, what Bereiter and Scardemelia (1982) call "knowledge telling" of predefined information, students may generate their own ideas.

High school students who wrote extended, open-ended journals over a period of time produced final essays with higher levels of interpretation than did students who answered short-answer questions or who did no writing at all (Marshall 1984). In this same study, students who did no writing about texts did better than those responding to the short-answer questions, which is a typical required response. Marshall argues that these short-answer questions about different aspects of the text may fragment students' focus on synthesizing their ideas of a particular hypothesis or idea about the text.

Students' motivation to extend their response can be enhanced by even such subtle matters as how a question is worded. Students who were asked to write their own opinions about a text wrote significantly longer essays at a higher level of interpretation than did students who were assigned a definite topic (Newell 1986).

Dialogue-journal writing. Students improve in their ability to elaborate their responses when they receive feedback (in writing, on tape, or in a conference) from a teacher or peer that helps them perceive alternative ways of elaborating or organizing their writing (Staton 1980). In reacting with responses and questions based on certain heuristics, a teacher or peer is indirectly demonstrating strategies for extending and elaborating thinking.

Oral thinking-aloud. In giving oral "think-alouds," students respond with their "slow-motion" thoughts, as they are reading a poem or section of a story, to a teacher or peer or into a tape recorder. (One helpful prompt for eliciting the think-alouds is to ask students to think of themselves as sports commentators describing their own thought processes while reading.) Lytle (1982) found that over time, as students became more confident in their ability to express themselves, their responses became more elaborate.

Question-Asking and Problem-Finding Discussion Tasks

One incentive that impels students to go beyond initial responses is the need to cope with cognitive dissonance created by puzzling questions or aspects of a text they don't understand—for example, why a character did something bizarre. Having students bring their own questions or "things they didn't understand" to a discussion endows that discussion with purpose—to unravel and resolve the dissonance. One variation of this is the "author's chair" (Hansen 1983) in which one student assumes the role of the author and other students in the group pose questions to the "author." Students can also list questions or problems on the board and then base their discussion on those questions or problems rather than simply relying on the teacher's questions.

Role playing. After selecting a specific scene from a text, students in small groups could adopt the roles of different characters who must discuss a dilemma or conflict in the text or in their own lives (basing the role play on a conflict assumes that students will adopt conflicting perspectives, something that sustains the role play). After the role play is completed, students discuss how they felt in their roles and share any new insights about the characters' attributes and goals they gained from the role play. Students could also videotape their role play and use the tape for their follow-up discussion.

Learning literature by writing it. By integrating reading and writing instruction, students learn that constructing the meaning of texts and constructing their own texts involve many of the same generating, planning, reviewing, and revising processes (Pearson and Tierney 1984). In writing and revising stories or poems, students must define their intentions and then determine the extent to which their text fulfills their intentions. In doing so, they are learning the literary conventions of intentionality—that writers deliberately employ techniques to imply meanings. And, in developing a sense of what's involved in writing a story, they may develop some appreciation for literature as an art.

Features of Guided Response Activities

Once teachers understand how guided activities help students learn to use certain strategies, frames, scaffolds, or text structures, and how prior knowledge/experience helps students to understand texts, they could then develop activities containing the following features:

1. *Sequenced tasks.* Guided activities consist of a series of sequenced response tasks based on a set of strategies, each task building on previous tasks. An activity could begin with engaging or describing strategies, involving the tasks of listing images in a poem as well as emotional associations with those images. After listing images in a poem, a student reviews the list in order to define different patterns implied by the images.

2. *Teacher- or student-defined goals.* Depending on the ability level of the student, either the teacher or the student or both may define the goal or purpose of the activity.

3. *Open-ended responses.* Students are asked to give written open-ended responses to texts, encouraging them to make their own original responses rather than provide "correct answers."

4. *Preparation for a final project.* In some cases, the response tasks can stand alone, for example, as a journal entry. Or, the response tasks may be used to prepare students to complete a final project—an essay or a group discus-

sion—the tasks serving as "prewriting" to develop material necessary for successful completion of these projects.

5. *Systematic use of inference strategies.* The questions and response tasks are based on logical sequencing of inference strategies in which initial strategies (engaging, connecting, describing) may serve to develop information for subsequent strategies (interpreting, judging). As a result, students learn to extend their responses by relating strategies to each other, for example, connecting previous experience and the text in order to interpret that text.

6. *Tasks organized according to text-structure frames.* The response tasks may also be organized according to text-structure frames such as "opinion/example," "problem/solution," and "comparison/contrast."

7. *Reviewing and self-monitoring.* After completing each task, students review and assess their responses in order to prepare for subsequent response tasks. In contrast to completing worksheets, students monitor and integrate different responses according to an overall effort, tasks that may enhance their metacognitive abilities. High-achieving high school students are significantly more likely than low-achieving students to employ certain self-regulated learning strategies such as goal-setting, self-monitoring, and reviewing material (Zimmerman and Pons 1986).

8. *Relating knowledge, attitudes, and experience to the text.* Students are often asked to define their own knowledge, attitudes, and experience as they relate to the text. For example, if students are reading a story about a grandmother, they could write about their own perceptions of their grandparent(s) and compare their perceptions of their own grandparent(s) to the character in the text.

9. *Built-in examples.* Along with specific directions for how to complete tasks and the purpose for those tasks, students may also be given examples demonstrating successful use of a certain strategy.

10. *Collaborative efforts.* Students could work in pairs or small groups to complete these activities. In some cases, each student would assume a certain role or set of responsibilities. For example, if a group is writing and producing a video version of a short story, one student could be the director; another, the "camera-person"; and another, a writer. The guided activities should provide students with enough direction and structure so that each student can define his or her own unique responsibilities.

11. *Variations according to students' ability.* In constructing guided activities, a teacher varies the difficulty level and the specificity of response tasks according to students' ability levels. For example, a teacher may provide more specific tasks for less able learners who need more direction, and more global tasks for those who need less direction.

147

Completing the specific tasks may bolster poorer readers' self-esteem by giving them a sense of themselves as readers who can effectively employ certain strategies. Rather than attribute poorer readers' problems to "assumptions of defect" (permanent sensory or physiological problems) or "assumptions of deficiency" (lack of "skills"), Johnston and Winograd (1985) argue that poorer readers' problems stem from their sense of themselves as "failures" in their ability to employ certain reading strategies. In contrast, better readers are able confidently and efficiently to employ strategies geared toward achieving certain defined goals (Winograd 1984). Better readers are also better able to accurately assess and monitor their use of strategies in terms of fulfilling or not fulfilling their own goals. Poorer readers often inaccurately attribute their difficulty to their own lack of effort, ability, or to poor teaching. Rather than perceiving themselves as able to deal effectively with things they don't understand, they are overwhelmed by a text.

Teachers may reinforce poorer readers' low sense of efficacy by giving them the "correct answer" to questions, shifting the question to other students, giving them less "wait time" to answer questions, or attributing their difficulties to lack of effort. In contrast, if students are able to successfully complete certain tasks and are rewarded for completing those tasks, they may develop a sense of their own efficacy as competent readers.

In devising guided activities for poorer readers, teachers select strategies and tasks oriented toward achieving a clearly defined goal that poses little difficulty for students, providing these students with some clearly defined opportunity to succeed in a task.

Evaluation of Literary Responses

Functions of Evaluation

Evaluation should promote growth or change in students' responses—growth that occurs through assessing and revising their own responses. Evaluating the use of "informal" writing tasks such as journal entries, jotting, listing, mapping, and free-writing, tasks that involve tentative, exploratory, subjective, and often contradictory thinking, requires a different form of evaluation than does evaluation of more "formal" final essays in which coherence and logical organization take precedence. Evaluating informal writing focuses more on the degree to which students use writing to generate or explore meanings, whereas evaluation of more formal writing focuses on such criteria as coherence, relevancy, and use of evidence.

Evaluation should be "criterion-based" rather than "norm-based." Instead of being evaluated according to their performance relative to group norms, students should be evaluated according to their own individual growth in their use of response strategies based on clearly-defined criteria—a student's amount of writing, use of certain strategies, elaboration of ideas, and degree of insight. For example, in evaluating the students' use of "connecting" strategies, a teacher could assess the students' ability to specify the relationship between the text and other similar texts and to use that connection to interpret the text.

As a course progresses, a teacher may note changes in a student's ability to employ strategies. Rather than evaluating students relative to the group, a teacher is evaluating students against themselves, noting, for example, improvements in their ability to connect their own experiences to the text, an ability that further enhances their self-esteem as competent readers and writers.

Types of Evaluation Techniques

Teachers can evaluate students using a range of different evaluation techniques: taped or written comments on guided task forms or conferences with students. Or, they can teach peers to respond to each other's responses, for example, through exchange of journals or by observing each other's classroom responses. Teachers could use four basic evaluation strategies:

- *describing/reinforcing* use of specific inference strategies in order to bolster students' sense of competence, provide them with a vocabulary for conceiving their own response processes, and to prepare them for judging;
- *judging* students' responses using criteria such as sufficiency, relevancy, validity, insightfulness, and originality—criteria that vary according to the purposes of a task;
- *predicting changes or potential development*; and
- *monitoring and rewarding changes*.

In addition, teachers also attempt to *explain* students' responses in terms of the students' attitudes, knowledge, cognitive level, reading ability, orientation ("story-driven" vs. "point-driven"), and so forth. By explaining why students responded as they did, teachers can temper their judgments accordingly.

By providing effective evaluation, a teacher is demonstrating to students how to self-assess—how to describe, judge, and predict changes or potential development in their own responses.

Decision-Making Processes for Guided Activities: An Example

In order to illustrate the decision-making processes involved in devising guided activities, I will discuss my decisions in devising an activity for the poem "Missing Lips," by Phoebe Hanson (1974).

149

MISSING LIPS

My lips threaten to run away
To disappear without a trace
To fall down my mouth forever.

Wait, I cry. Don't leave me.
I stab at them with my lipstick,
Try to make them understand.

Leave us alone, they answer.
We want to go away
To a warmer climate for the winter.

Go then, I scream.
See how you do without me.
See if you find someone to feed you.

They fly south on my credit cards,
Charge hotels and meals in Fort Lauderdale,
Swim suits and lounge robes in Palm Springs.

In March they return,
Juicy and brassy,
Talking too much,
Even to strangers in elevators
Who look at the floor indicators and
Try not to notice.

They kiss far too often that summer,
Multitudes of mouths on tennis courts and in cloakrooms.
But none seem to move them
Out of their terrible insolence.

I try to ignore them.
They are getting out of hand.
I feed them nothing but lip gloss for months.

They take off on a Greyhound bus,
Work as waitresses, mouth off to truckdrivers
Who complain about weeping meringues on lemon pies.

I go after them in my Volkswagen,
Plead with them to return
To finish high school.

Leave us alone, they pout.
Give us our own room with color T.V.
Stop asking us where we spend our nights and when
We might come back.

Get in the car, I say.
We'll talk about it as we drive.
Sulking and mumbling in the back seat,
They press tightly together . . . say nothing more all the way home.

"Unpacking" My Own Inference Processes. In order to identify strategies students may find useful in responding to the poem, I think about my own responses and the strategies I employ:

- *engaging*: my empathy for the lips' carefree, happy-go-lucky attitude toward life without responsibilities versus my distancing from the lips' irresponsibility;
- *describing*: my perception of the lips' and the "I's" acts that imply different traits, beliefs, and goals;
- *connecting*: my own experience of conflict between the conventional and the unconventional with the conflict between the lips and the "I"; and
- *interpreting*: the lips represent one side of the "I's" personality—the romantic, unconventional, "id" side, which the more rational, conventional, "superego" side is attempting to control.

Anticipating Possible Student Responses. I then think about how my students may respond. I suspect that they will be interested in the differences between the lips and the "I." In order to define those differences, they will need to describe certain consistent aspects of the lips' and the "I's" actions in order to inductively infer traits, beliefs, and goals. I also sense that in order to understand the differences between the symbolic nature of the lips and the "I," students may need to relate their own autobiographical experience with inner conflicts to the poem.

Defining the Overall Purpose of the Activity. This refers to what strategies or heuristics I want the students to acquire—for example, the ability to explain a character's action in terms of beliefs and goals.

In this case, I would like students to be able to link information about the lips and the "I" according to consistent patterns to enable them to inductively define and compare these patterns. I then want them to relate their own experience of inner conflict or conflict with others with the symbolic conflict between the lips and the "I."

Determining a Final Outcome (if any). Here I would consider an essay, journal entry, role play, and so forth. I want students to write about their perceptions of the lips and the "I," relating their own perceptions about their experience to the poem.

Selecting and Sequencing Strategies. After determining the final outcome, I would select and sequence those strategies and review tasks that may best fulfill my purpose and prepare students to fulfill the final outcome.

In considering an appropriate sequence of tasks, I decide to have students first describe the lips' and the "I's" behavior in order to prepare them for inferring traits and beliefs. I then have them connect their inferences about the lips and the "I" to their own experience with conflict between dream and reality to conflict in the text.

Selecting Tasks. Certain tasks (listing, mapping, free-writing, etc.—Gere 1985) are most appropriate for fulfilling certain strategies. For example, nonstop rush-writing or free-writing works well for evoking related autobiographical experiences; listing, for generating items; or mapping, for describing relationships between characters.

I selected a listing task for describing the lips' and the "I's" actions (see below) to help students perceive certain patterns in the lists. In order that they connect their experience to the text, I also have the students think about their own fantasy/escape dreams and the relationship of those dreams to their self-concept.

Formatting the Activity. This involves using white space, subheads, parallel lists, and so forth. By numbering lists, students may be encouraged to list more than one or two things. Or by using parallel lists, students may infer relationships or differences between the information listed.

Based on these decisions, I constructed the following activity:

1. Read over the poem several times.
2. List the things that the lips and the "I" do:

The lips' behaviors:	*The "I's" behaviors:*
a.	a.
b.	b.
c.	c.
d.	d.
e.	e.
f.	f.

3. In order to understand people, we try to perceive patterns or consistent behaviors. Read back over your lists in #2 and infer what these behaviors suggest about the lips and the "I's" traits or attitudes, for example, that the "I" is "angry."

The lips' traits and beliefs: *The "I's" traits and beliefs:*

a.   a.

b.   b.

c.   c.

d.   d.

4. Based on what you wrote in #2 and #3, write in your journal or discuss in a small group what you believe to be the differences between the lips and the "I."

5. Now, in your journal, write about the following:

a. List some traits or beliefs that best describe yourself.

b. If you could do anything you always dreamed of doing, what would you do?

c. Is there any conflict between your own traits and beliefs and your dream? Is that conflict similar to that experienced by the "I" and the lips?

6. In your journal, write about any of the following:

a. If you were to invite both the "I" and the lips—as two separate persons—to your party, how would they behave?

b. In what ways are you similar to or different from the "I" in the poem?

c. Do you have your own "lips" to contend with?

d. How would you judge the "I" and the lips?

Benefits of Guided Activities for the Teacher

A number of benefits in using these guided activities justify the initial time investment required to develop the activities.

1. *Improved final essays.* If the guided activities are used as prewriting tasks for final essays, students are able to develop information and formulate ideas that may improve the quality of final essays. In our own research (Reilly, Beach, and Crabtree 1986), students who completed guided activity tasks prior to writing final essays, when compared with students who did not complete the same tasks, wrote final essays judged as higher in quality.

2. *Improved discussion and collaboration.* Completing writing tasks prior to small- or large-group discussion may help students formulate their

thoughts in a systematic manner, often ensuring that they have something to contribute to the discussion.

Having students complete the activities in collaborative small groups also improves students' ability to work with each other. Students responding to poems in collaborative learning groups wrote more mature post-test poetry interpretations than did students in teacher-led discussion groups (Straw 1986).

3. *Structure for students who need structure.* In large classes, teachers often have difficulty providing individual attention to students whose learning styles require more direction or structure than teachers have time to provide. Guided activities, while not a substitute for teacher attention, do provide some structured tasks for these students.

4. *Strategies for poor readers.* As previously noted, one characteristic of poor readers is their lack of strategies for understanding texts. By completing guided activities, they are incidentally internalizing a set of heuristics or strategies, which presumably enhances their confidence in their ability to make inferences in a systematic manner.

5. *Students' self-assessment.* Guided activities encourage students to review and assess their performance in terms of sufficiency, relevancy, validity, value, and insightfulness. By learning to assess their own responses, they may recognize and attempt to deal with limitations in their responses, thus bolstering their metacomprehension skills.

6. *Diagnosis and assessment.* Because the teacher knows the strategies included in an activity, he or she can readily diagnose students' difficulties or assess students' performance on specific responses. They can also assess final products in terms of performance on prerequisite tasks.

7. *Involvement of parents.* Parents want to help students with homework activities, but they often don't have a clear idea as to what the teacher expects the students to do. The specific instructions and demonstrations in guided activities may assist parents in helping students with homework assignments.

8. *Conversion to computer.* Guided activities could also be converted to computer-guided tasks, which may enhance their appeal to certain students. One example of a guided story-writing computer-based activity is *Writing a Narrative* (MECC). Authoring systems can assist teachers in converting guided activities to a computer format. Or, teachers can use word-processing programs to store generic tasks and demonstration responses.

9. *Students constructing activities for other students.* When students construct activities for other students, they are often highly motivated because they have a defined purpose and audience for deciding on appropriate tasks.

10. *Coordination of instruction, diagnosis, and student performance.* As illustrated below, by coordinating classroom instruction with activity tasks, teachers can base decisions about instruction on a diagnosis of students' per-

formance. A teacher may select only those strategies in which students have received instruction. However, if students are having difficulty completing a particular task, for example, inferring characters' beliefs, a teacher may then want to give more instruction in or demonstration of that strategy.

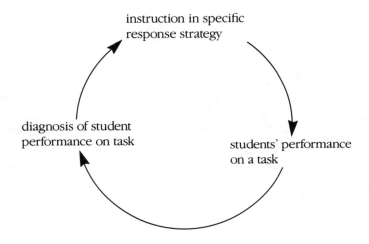

instruction in specific
response strategy

students' performance
on a task

diagnosis of student
performance on task

To summarize, this chapter describes a particular approach to instruction that is highly consistent with the concept of strategic teaching. This approach elaborates ways in which the teacher may mediate learning by helping the learner construct meaning from text. Specifically, these activities guide students (1) to link new information to prior knowledge, (2) to use organizational patterns (frames, logical plans, and text structures) to direct and extend their thinking, and (3) to develop a repertoire of inference and response strategies. Further, teachers continually alter their instruction based on diagnosis of student performance. These themes are applied in an extended example showing the decision-making processes involved in applying this approach to a specific sequence of instruction. By acquiring the strategies discussed (and listed in Figure 7.2), students should enhance their understanding of literature.

Figure 7.2. Catalogue: Response Strategies for Assignments

Engaging

1. EMPATHIZES/IDENTIFIES/GETS INVOLVED
Reader adopts character's perspective/relates positively to the character or world of text.

2. RESPONDS EMOTIONALLY
Reader responds or reacts emotionally or cites emotional associations to the events, language, or characters.

Connecting

3. RELATES AUTOBIOGRAPHICAL EXPERIENCE TO TEXT
Reader describes similar or related experiences or persons in relationship to events or characters in the text. These autobiographical responses help trigger related knowledge or attitudes that may assist in interpreting the text.

4. TRANSPORTS CHARACTERS OR TEXTS INTO ANOTHER "WHAT-IF" CONTEXT OR SELF AS READER INTO THE WORLD OF THE TEXT
Reader places characters or text into "real-world" or hypothetical contexts. For example, students are given a specific, familiar setting, and are asked questions as to how certain characters from the text would behave in that setting.

5. RELATES ATTITUDES TO TEXT
Reader defines own related attitudes and compares or contrasts those attitudes with those of the characters or author. Students could write about their own attitudes or they could complete various attitude scales (rating attitude statements, rank ordering concepts, etc.) in reference to themselves or to the characters or world of the text.

6. RELATES KNOWLEDGE OF WORLD TO TEXT
Reader defines own knowledge about the world and relates it to the text.

7. RELATES TEXT TO SIMILAR TEXTS
Reader describes a text, film, or television program that is similar to the text.

Describing

8. DESCRIBES INFORMATION ABOUT CHARACTERS' ACTS, TRAITS, BELIEFS, PLANS, GOALS, RELATIONSHIPS, EVENTS, OR SETTING
Reader lists, jots, logs, free-associates, and so forth, specific information about the text.

9. LINKS OR CLUSTERS WORDS, CONCEPTS, IMAGES, ACTIONS
Reader links, connects, maps, or clusters aspects of the text according to similarity of meaning.

Interpreting

10. INFERS/EXPLAINS CHARACTERS' ACTS
Reader explains characters' acts by using information about traits, beliefs, plans, or goals.

11. INFERS AUTHOR'S OR CHARACTERS' INTENTIONS
Reader infers that an author is deliberately using certain language or employing certain techniques to convey certain meanings.

12. INFERS THE CHARACTERS' OR NARRATOR'S PERSPECTIVE OR WORLD VIEW
Reader infers the nature of a character's or narrator's perspective or world view—how they conceive of others, themselves, and the world.

13. INFERS SOCIAL NORMS, CONVENTIONS, OR VALUE ASSUMPTIONS
Based on information about the characters' actions, beliefs, or perspectives, a reader infers certain norms, conventions, or value assumptions constituting appropriate/inappropriate behavior in a certain place, setting, or world.

14. INFERS A POINT OR THEME
Based on inferences about social norms, conventions, or value assumptions, a reader infers a point or theme. Having inferred that a character has violated certain conventions, a reader can infer what the character has learned from that violation.

15. GENERALIZES TO A PROTOTYPE, SYMBOL, ARCHETYPE, OR IDEA
Reader infers that the characters or story line are representative of a prototype, archetype, or idea, and gives reasons why the characters or story represents a certain type.

16. MAKES PREDICTIONS
Reader predicts subsequent events, outcomes, or endings based on his or her perceptions of certain patterns implying consistent character behavior. A reader then reviews the text in order to give reasons for the prediction.

17. ASKS QUESTIONS ABOUT THE TEXT
Reader poses questions about the text, questions that can encourage further thinking about a text.

18. DEFINES DIFFICULTIES IN UNDERSTANDING
Readers define what it is that they don't understand and give reasons why they don't understand the text, reasons that serve as schema for reviewing the text to find helpful information to improve their understanding.

Judging

19. JUDGES CHARACTERS
Reader judges characters according to such criteria as insightfulness, diplomacy, and appearance, according to assumptions or norms operating within the world of the text.

20. JUDGES THE QUALITY OF TEXTS
Reader judges the quality or worth of a text by using criteria such as style, organization, and characterization.

References

Applebee, A. *Contexts for Learning to Write*. Hillsdale, N.J.: Ablex, 1986.

Applebee, A., and J. Langer. "Instructional Scaffolding: Reading and Writing as Natural Language Activities." In *Composing and Comprehending*, edited by J. Jensen. Urbana, Ill.: National Council of Teachers of English, 1984.

Beach, R., and D. Appleman. "Reading Strategies for Expository and Literary Text Types." In *Becoming Readers in a Complex Society, 83d Yearbook of the National Society for the Study of Education*, edited by A. Purves and O. Niles. Chicago: National Society for the Study of Education, 1984.

Beach, R., and L. Wendler. "Development Differences in Responding to a Short Story." *Research in the Teaching of English* (in press).

Beck, I., R. Omanson, and M. McKeown. "An Instructional Redesign of Reading Lesson: Effects on Comprehension." *Reading Research Quarterly* 17 (1982): 462-481.

Bereiter, C., and M. Scardamalia. "From Conversation to Composition: The Role of Instruction in a Developmental Process." In *Advances in Instructional Psychology*, Vol. 2, edited by R. Glaser. Hillsdale, N.J.: Erbaum Press.

Bleich, D. *Readings and Feelings*. Urbana, Ill.: National Council of Teachers of English, 1981.

Brown, A., and A. Palincsar. "Inducing Strategic Learning from Text by Means of Informed, Self-control Training." *Topics in Learning and Learning Disabilities* 2 (1982): 1-17.

Bracewell, R., C. Frederiksen, and J. Frederiksen. "Cognitive Processes in Composing and Comprehending Discourse." *Educational Psychologist* 17 (1982): 146-164.

Bruce, B., and A. Rubin. "Strategies for Controlling Hypothesis Formation in Reading." In *Promoting Reading Comprehension*, edited by J. Flood. Newark, Del.: International Reading Association, 1984.

Culler, J. *Structuralist Poetics: Structuralism, Linguistics, and the Study of Literature.* Ithaca, N.Y.: Cornell University Press, 1975.

Galda, L. "Assessment: Responses to Literature." In *Secondary School Reading: What Research Reveals for Classroom Practice,* edited by A. Berger and H. Robinson. Urbana, Ill.: ERIC/RCS, 1982.

Gere, A. *Roots in the Sawdust.* Urbana, Ill.: National Council of Teachers of English, 1985.

Gordon, C., and C. Braun. "Using Story Schema as an Aid to Reading and Writing." *Reading Teacher* 37 (1983): 116-121.

Hansen, J. "Authors Respond to Authors." *Language Arts* 60 (1983): 176-183.

Hanson, P. "Missing Lips." In *Minnesota Poets #1,* edited by Seymour Yesner. Minneapolis, Minn.: Nodin Press, 1974.

Hare, V., and K. Borchard. "Direct Instruction in Summarization Skills." *Reading Research Quarterly* 20 (1984): 62-78.

Heath, S. "Being Literate in America: A Sociohistorical Perspective." In *Issues in Literacy: A Research Perspective, 34th Yearbook of the National Reading Conference,* edited by J. Niles and R. Lalik. Rochester, N.Y.: The National Reading Conference, 1985.

Iser, I. *The Act of Reading.* Baltimore: John Hopkins Press, 1978.

Jacobsen, M. "Looking for Literary Space: The Willing Suspension of Disbelief Revisited." *Research in the Teaching of English* 16 (1982): 21-38.

Johnston, P., and P. Winograd. "Passive Failure in Reading." *Journal of Reading Behavior* 27 (1985): 279-302.

Jones, B. "Response Instruction." In *Reading, Thinking, and Concept Development,* edited by T. Harris and E. Cooper. New York: The College Board, 1985.

Langer, J. "Examining Background Knowledge and Text Comprehension." *Reading Research Quarterly* 4 (1984): 468-481.

Lytle, S. "Exploring Comprehension Style: A Study of Twelfth Grade Readers' Transactions with Texts." Doctoral diss., Stanford University, 1982.

Mason, J. "Lesson Repair Techniques for Teaching Comprehension Techniques." Paper presented at the annual meeting of the National Reading Conference, Austin, 1983.

Mason, J. and K. Au. *Reading Instruction for Today.* Glenview, Ill.: Scott, Foresman, 1986.

Marshall, J. "The Effects of Writing on Students' Understanding of Literary Texts." Paper presented at the annual meeting of the National Council of Teachers of English, Detroit, 1984.

Meyer, B. *The Organization of Prose and its Effects on Memory.* Amsterdam: North-Holland, 1975.

Newell, G., K. Suszynski, and R. Weingart. "The Effects of Writing in a Reader-based Versus Text-based Mode on Students' Understanding of Two Short Stories." Paper presented at the annual meeting of the American Educational Research Association, San Francisco, 1986.

Palinscar, A., and A. Brown. "Reciprocal Teaching: Activities to Promote 'Reading with Your Mind'." In *Reading, Thinking, and Concept Development,* edited by T. Harris and E. Cooper. New York: The College Board, 1985.

Pearson, P. D., and R. Tierney. "On Becoming a Thoughtful Reader: Learning to Read Like a Writer." In *Becoming Readers in a Complex Society, 84th Yearbook of the National Society for the Study of Education,* edited by A. Purves and O. Niles. Chicago: National Society for the Study of Education, 1984.

Petrosky, A. "From Story to Essay: Reading and Writing." *College Composition and Communication* 33 (1982): 19-36.

Purves, A., and R. Beach. *Literature and the Reader: Research on Response to Literature, Reading Interests, and Teaching of Literature*. Urbana, Ill.: National Council of Teachers of English, 1972.

Reilly, J., R. Beach, and L. Crabtree. "The Effects of Guided Inference Instruction on Students' Writing Skills." Paper presented at the annual meeting of the American Educational Research Association, San Francisco, 1986.

Schank, R. *Dynamic Memory: A Theory of Learning in Computers and People*. Cambridge: Cambridge University Press, 1982.

Staton, J. "Writing and Counseling: Using a Dialogue Journal." *Language Arts* 57 (1980): 514-518.

Stein, N., and C. Glenn. "An Analysis of Story Comprehension in Elementary School Children." In *New Directions in Discourse Processing*, Vol. 2 in *Advances in Discourse Processes*, edited by R. Freedle. Norwood, N.J.: Ablex Publishing.

Straw, S. "Collaborative Learning and Reading for Theme in Poetry." Paper presented at the annual meeting of the National Council of Teachers of English, San Antonio, 1986.

Strickland, D., and J. Feeley. "Using Children's Concept of Story to Improve Reading and Writing." In *Reading, Thinking, and Concept Development*, edited by T. Harris and E. Cooper. New York: The College Board, 1985.

Svensson, C. *The Construction of Poetic Meaning*. Uppsala, Sweden: Liber Press, 1985.

Vipond, D., and R. Hunt. "Point-drive Understanding: Pragmatic and Cognitive Dimensions of Literary Reading." *Poetics* 13 (1984): 261-277.

Winograd, P. "Strategic Difficulties in Summarizing Texts." *Reading Research Quarterly* 19 (1984): 404-425.

Zimmerman, B., and M. Pons. "Development of a Structured Interview for Assessing Student Use of Self-Regulated Learning Strategies." *American Educational Research Journal* 23 (1986): 614-629.

The Editors

Conclusions

The major thesis of this book is that good instruction needs to be grounded in what is known about learning and that both teaching and learning are processes that can be considered across content areas. For too long, most considerations of teaching have been confined to a particular content area. Additionally, with the focus on content, little attention has been directed to what strategies students need to employ in order to learn a specific curriculum and what teachers can do to help students learn how to learn.

It has been our design in this volume to begin our inquiry concerning teaching at a new point—with a discussion of the current research in learning. From that perspective, considering what students need to be able to do in order to learn content, we moved to a review of what is known about good instruction and drew the important parallels for planning, executing, and evaluating instruction. The model of strategic teaching that we propose highlights the importance of the teaching/learning connections.

This model also makes clear the extremely complex thinking process that teaching is. Strategic teaching requires achieving a balance between what the students bring to learning and what the content goals are. It means balancing the teaching of content with the teaching of strategies that students need to use in order to learn that content well. It also means matching the level of presentation of new content with the final outcomes desired so that over time students become able to deal with the material in useful and meaningful ways. For many teachers, strategic teaching also means balancing their need to guide student learning by providing scaffolded instruction with their goal of student independence. In all cases, strategic teaching places the teacher in a central role as planner and mediator of learning. The numerous factors that are realities in classrooms cannot be homogenized and reduced in teaching manuals and instructional programs. Good teachers are continually actively assessing students' knowledge, levels of motivation, and interest; evaluating the materials for instruction and the presentation of content to build the best learning; and modifying instruction based on feedback from the ongoing class learning.

The power of this framework for providing a common tool for the discussion and development of better instruction across curriculum areas was then explored by experts in four content areas. Their insights certainly provide much meat for continuous dialogue and reflection on content learning using components highlighted within this framework.

In the first of these content chapters, Anderson presents a compelling example of why it is so important for teachers to begin instruction with an understanding of their students' prior knowledge assumptions. If scientific misconceptions are not addressed directly, even "good teaching" becomes a waste of time. Anderson's development of an instructional process beginning with the identification of the misconception and then leading students to work through to a more adequate scientific understanding parallels the general strategic teaching model proposed in Part I of the book. He clearly demonstrates how the instructional process model presented in Planning Guide 3 in Part I can be used by science educators to develop strategic learning for conceptual change.

Anderson's description of instructional conditions for bringing about conceptual change presents a good frame for other content disciplines. Indeed, his Planning Guide may be applied directly to any instruction that might involve conceptual change. We would do well to consider how we as teachers establish dissatisfaction with existing misconceptions, and make the new conception intelligible, plausible, and applicable to a variety of new situations or problems. What science educators have learned about the process of teaching to produce conceptual change can be instructive to all of us who are interested in helping students relate new information and concepts to their prior knowledge assumptions.

Another point that emerges from Anderson's work is the difficulty of adapting instruction to meet the needs of all students. Frequently instruction in science benefits only the classroom's high achievers. An awareness of the strategies described in this volume can lead to adaptations in instructional approaches and methods that respond to the abilities, attentiveness, and educational needs of a broader range of students. It may well be, however, that further research, which goes beyond current conceptual explanation, will have to develop additional techniques and approaches that are more responsive to the needs of all students, especially passive learners and those with learning problems.

Alvermann, in her chapter on social studies learning, deals directly with the problems of diversity in classrooms. Using the process model presented in Part I, she presents specific examples of instructional materials teachers can use to differentiate assignments and outcome activities for students at different levels of knowledge and ability. These examples also clarify her point: that the field of social studies education is concerned with the development of thinking abilities—in all students. The illustrations she provides present concrete examples of how teachers can scaffold instruction to meet the needs of all students in that developmental process.

After relating issues in social studies education to the basic considerations about learning outlined in Part I, Alvermann provides us with a helpful example of how a teacher could use the strategic teaching Planning Guides to prepare instruction to meet students' learning needs. Her specific instructional activities should prove helpful to teachers in implementing this process approach to learning within their own content area .

Lindquist's consideration of math education picks up on the same themes expressed by others in the volume; concepts relating to strategic teaching and learning and cognitive instruction are integral to math learning. Students need to be active, thoughtful learners to make sense of mathematics and make it more than just memorization of tables and steps in mechanical solutions. The metacognitive aspects of learning come clearly to the fore in her discussion of the directions being explored now in math education. Students' self-perceptions as math learners and users are intricately involved with their active awareness and involvement in learning. This theme had not been addressed as clearly in the other chapters, and is certainly an important one for all content learning. Just as the importance of clarifying misconceptions is at the heart of science education, research on the importance of dealing with the personal affective involvement of students with content is most clearly identified in math education.

All of these ideas are integrated and applied in her excellent examples of strategic teaching in mathematics. In each example, one can see the interplay of content expertise and knowledge of how students learn as she anticipates student responses to the instruction and guides students in and out of difficult learning contexts. Her examples also show the range of applications of strategic teaching across the different grade levels.

In the chapter on literature, as with the other content subjects, Beach also sees the need to involve students in a response to the subject matter as a basic goal of literature instruction. By stimulating such responses, students are encouraged to develop critical thinking and direct participation in the process of comprehension. All activities focus on generating a response to the literary work. These activities require students to make inferences and interpret text at a high level of abstraction. In order to accomplish this frequently challenging task, students must develop the ability to draw upon prior knowledge about experience and strategy usage. A teacher's preliminary scaffolding of instruction, often best accomplished through preliminary guided activities, can encourage more autonomous responsiveness on the part of students. Beach provides clear support for teachers who want to reflect on their own instruction and build a wider repertoire of ways of engaging students with literature.

Additionally, Beach's focus on response instruction is interesting for two reasons. First, much of his instruction involves linking what is read to prior knowledge after the act of reading. Second, it is still relatively rare that content teachers provide explicit strategy instruction to help students construct responses to written assignments.

Beach, Lindquist, and Alvermann all present some important "think alouds" about how teachers plan for content teaching. It is clear that, given the complexity of factors that influence cognitive instruction, strategic teachers do not rely on prepared materials and guides for instruction. They begin as content experts who examine the materials, make decisions about outcomes, and then design instructional activities to match their students' needs for linking to prior knowledge, strategy development, and affective involvement in learning. Like Mrs. Sampson, each author plans for extended sequences of instruction that form a conceptual unit, and provides instruction for each of the phases of learning.

These descriptions also illustrate the complexity and diversity of the role of the teacher as mediator across the disciplines. The strategic teacher is a mediator of instruction, providing opportunities for students to become independent in all subject areas. The effort is not the teacher's alone; nor is it entirely the student's. They work together, like master and apprentice, with the teacher providing the intellectual scaffolding, tools, and project, and the student applying his or her talents, acquired skills, and willingness to learn and work. In this joint venture, content drives instruction—the task at hand provides the rudiments of the plan and method. The teacher must also be attentive to how the particular student makes connections within the subject area and uses strategies responsively.

Strategies and scaffolding are useful for all students because the design of strategies considers the various degrees to which students explore meaning. They can be varied according to ability by specific response tasks. Strategies provide defined goals and a range of guidance and evaluation for students—especially for the large number of less proficient readers who need the reinforcement that comes from a sense of accomplishment and success. This, in turn, complements and enhances the cognitive benefits of these strategies and activities, resulting in improved work as students develop the ability to monitor their learning independently.

Throughout both parts of this book, consistent themes emerge that substantiate the great opportunity that presents itself now for all educators in all disciplines interested in improving students' thinking and learning to dialogue together and prepare schoolwide plans to those ends. Using a common language and research base permits greater communication. Our hope is that the specific discipline-based examinations of learning and instruction presented in Part II will confirm for you the commonalities that exist across content areas and provide an impetus for the dialogue that is needed.

Our goal in writing this book was to stimulate reflection on how we as educators are preparing students to become thoughtful learners, capable of and interested in pursuing learning both within and beyond schooling. The thrust of this framework has been to develop students' thinking by equipping them with strategies that put them in control of their own learning. This is accomplished by bringing to students' conscious attention what they need to know and providing them with strategies to pursue their goals.

Some teachers and administrators may view the information in this book as a confirmation of their beliefs because they are familiar with the philosophy and some of the strategies presented. For those of you in that situation, we hope that the text provides some support, encouragement, and new information and ideas to extend your efforts. For others, the ideas in this volume may represent new and challenging possibilities and directions. We hope that you will take the time to reflect on these ideas and allow yourself to be confronted by them. If you are wrestling with some of the ideas presented here, you may want to consider the following issues that emerge from this volume as they reflect on instructional development:

- What is your conception of learning and how can the research on learning guide your understanding of the process?

- What forms the foundation for instructional planning—is it a textbook, your content knowledge, or mandated outcomes?

- What strategies or approaches to learning do your students use regularly? Has anyone surveyed students' planning for and actual use of study strategies?

- What is the teacher's role in developing strategic approaches to learning? How can departments work together to achieve more active, thoughtful learners?

- What is the balance between content and strategy instruction in your school, and how are both evaluated?

- What model of instruction do you and your colleagues use in your teaching? Does it involve a process approach that takes into account preparation activities, active involvement during learning, and consolidation and application activities—with opportunities for reflection and nonlinear thinking?

- Do you consider the ways content disciplines organize knowledge and provide instruction so that your students, too, can become more conceptual and organized in their learning?

We hope that you will interact with the ideas presented, relating them to your prior conceptions of learning and teaching, comparing and contrasting where our conceptions are different, and then finding ways to accommodate some of the new information where appropriate. Finally, it is in the ongoing dialogue and application of ideas that we, as strategic learners and teachers, will test the merit of these concepts.

About the Editors and Authors

The Editors

Beau Fly Jones is Senior Associate, North Central Regional Educational Laboratory, Elmhurst, Illinois.

Annemarie Sullivan Palincsar is Assistant Professor, Department of Counseling, Educational Psychology, and Special Education, Michigan State University, East Lansing.

Donna Sederburg Ogle is Chair, Reading and Language Department, National College of Education, Evanston, Illinois.

Eileen Glynn Carr is Assistant Professor, Department of Teacher Education, Eastern Michigan University, Ypsilanti.

The Subject-Area Authors

Donna Alvermann is Associate Professor, Department of Reading Education, College of Education, University of Georgia, Athens.

Charles W. Anderson is Associate Professor, Department of Teacher Education, Michigan State University, East Lansing.

Richard Beach is Professor of English Education, Department of Curriculum and Instruction, University of Minnesota, Minneapolis.

Mary Montgomery Lindquist is Callaway Professor of Mathematics Education, Department of Curriculum and Instruction, School of Education, Columbus College, Columbus, Georgia.